GRUNDLAGE DEUTSCH 1

Fundamentals of German

Jessie G. McGuire

Walter G. O'Connell High School, Copiague, NY (retired)

Joseph Castine

Northport High School, Northport, NY (retired)

AMSCO SCHOOL PUBLICATIONS, INC.
315 Hudson Street / New York, NY 10013

Cover design by: A Good Thing, Inc.

Please visit our Web site at:
www.amscopub.com

When ordering this please specify *either* **R 63 W** *or*
GRUNDLAGE DEUTSCH 1: FUNDAMENTALS OF GERMAN

ISBN   978-1-56765-407-3

NYC Item   56765-407-2

1 2 3 4 5 6 7 8 9 10   12 11 10 09 08 07 06

Preface

Grundlage Deutsch 1 is designed as a review of the material covered in a typical first-level German course. It offers learners a chance to review, practice and strengthen their understanding of the German language within communicative contexts. Vocabulary has been limited to basic first-year language, so that *Grundlage Deutsch 1* may be used independently or as a supplement to any basal text.

ORGANIZATION

Grundlage Deutsch 1 consists of 12 chapters, each organized around a single major grammar concept. The base concept is explained succinctly and clearly, illustrated with usage examples, followed by relevant practice exercises for the learner, and then expanded upon. Each expansion explanation follows the same pattern of explanation, examples, and practice exercises. Chapters start with clear introductions to the new concept and expand in small increments until the required functions of the first-level German related to this concept have been introduced, illustrated and practiced.

VOCABULARY AND GRAMMAR

Grundlage Deutsch 1 is not a vocabulary enrichment workbook. Its goal is to offer students of any ability level an opportunity to strengthen their understanding and mastery of the functions needed to communicate in German. The book works with a limited, elementary core of vocabulary, which was chosen after reviewing several current German texts. The vocabulary is used and recycled into different situational contexts throughout the book. A German-English vocabulary list and numerous grammar charts are included for easy reference.

EXERCISES

Each grammar explanation is followed by a series of exercises. Exercises are based on communicative situations and develop a "story" throughout the chapter. They begin with simple recognition activities and scaffold toward more complex tasks. They progress from easy to more difficult in small, manageable steps that student can easily handle.

FLEXIBILITY

Grundlage Deutsch 1 can be used successfully whether students are working independently, in small learning groups, or in a classroom situation. Each chapter focuses on a single, or a few related grammar concepts. The vocabulary is limited to basic first-year glossaries, and the extensive table of contents allows learners to identify readily where explanations and exercises relevant to their needs can be found. It can be used independently or with little or no extra preparation as a classroom supplement to any basal level-one German text.

Mastering communicative functions gives learners confidence and a firm basis on which to continue building their knowledge of German. *Grundlage Deutsch 1* cements the essential skills necessary for mastery of level one and increases students' communicative abilities. Its gradual progression from simple to complex, review of previously learned concepts, clear explanations, and transparent organization make it ideal whether used as a classroom tool, a remedial tool, or an enrichment tool. We wish all learners *Viel Glück* as they work through the exercises in *Grundlage Deutsch 1* and look forward to welcoming everyone to level two.

Jessie McGuire and Joseph Castine

Contents

CHAPTER 1
Present Tense of Verbs

When speaking or writing German, all verbs must have an ending added to their stem to designate who or what is doing the action.

The infinitive is the form of the verb shown in word lists and dictionaries. The stem of the verb is formed by dropping the *-en* (or *–n* if there is no *–en*) from the infinitive.

geh-en	*to go*	**heiss-en**	*to be called*	**hör-en**	*to hear*
koch-en	*to cook*	**komm-en**	*to come*	**mach-en**	*to make/do*
sing-en	*to sing*	**spiel-en**	*to play*	**tanz-en**	*to dance*
tu-n	*to do*				

1. Formation of the Present Tense

The present tense is formed by adding the following endings to the verb stem:

SINGULAR	PLURAL
ich spiel – e *I play, I do play, I am playing*	**wir spiel – en** *we play, we do play, we are playing*
du spiel – st *you (informal) play, do play, are playing*	**ihr spiel – t** *you (informal) play, do play, are playing*
er, sie, es spiel – t *he, she, or it plays, does play, is playing*	**sie spiel – en** *they play, they do play, they are playing*
Sie spiel – en *you (formal) play, do play, are playing*	

ÜBUNG A | **Ein Klassenspiel.** You're playing a game in class. Your teacher calls out a person, and you have to say what they are doing at the moment.

EXAMPLE: Sabine / schreiben eine Arbeit   **Sabine schreibt eine Arbeit.**

1. Jakob und Stefan / hören Musik

   _____

2. du / spielen Schach mit Melanie

   _____

3. Dietmar / kochen Nudeln mit Tomatensoße

   _____

4. du und deine Freundin / sitzen in der Klasse

_____

5. Herr Lutz / singen ein Lied

_____

If the verb stem ends in –t, –d, or two consonants followed by an –n, add –e before the –st or –t in the _du, ihr,_ or _er/sie/es_ forms. This makes the resulting verb easier to pronounce.

Er arbeitet in der Schule. (arbeiten)	_He works in the school._
Sie findet ihr Buch nicht. (finden)	_She isn't finding her book._
Die Tür öffnet automatisch. (öffnen)	_The door opens automatically._
Er wartet in der Klasse. (warten)	_He's waiting in school._

ÜBUNG B | **Der erste Schultag.** You've finished a story about your first day at school, but you left the verb endings until you could check them at home. Complete the story.

EXAMPLE: Hans find__et__ seine Schuhe nicht.

Hallo! Ich heiss_____ Hans. Ich geh_____ zur Schule. Mein Bruder Josef komm_____ mit.

Er ist 16 Jahre alt und arbeit_____ für den Musiklehrer. Er lern_____ Spanisch und ich

lern_____ Deutsch. Wir sag_____ der Mutter „Tschüs!", öffn_____ die Tür und war_____

auf den Bus. Der Bus bring_____ uns zur Schule. Ich find_____ meine Klasse schnell. Josef

find_____ seine Klasse nicht.

2. Using the Present Tense

a. In English, there are three different forms of the present tense: "I play", "I do play" and "I am playing". In German, all three of these meanings are expressed in one tense: _ich spiele_. There is no change in the verb when the meaning changes from "I play" to "I am playing". If necessary for comprehension, an adverb of time may be added. Note that, although the English translation changes, the verb tense remains unchanged in the following conversation.

> **Spielst du Karten?** _Do you play cards?_
> **Ja, ich spiele Karten.** _Yes, I play cards._
> **Ich spiele Karten jetzt.** _I am playing cards now._

b. When combined with an adverb or adverbial phrase that implies futurity, the present tense may also be used to express future actions.

> **Der Chor singt nächste Woche.** *The Chorus will sing next week.*
> **Er kommt am Samstag mit.** *He will come along on Saturday.*

ÜBUNG C   **Das Schulorchester.** You are looking at a picture of the school orchestra and discussing it with your friend. Create the conversation.

EXAMPLE: Christina / spielen / Trompete   Christina **spielt** Trompete.

1. ich / spielen / Flöte

   _____

2. Helga und Peter / hören / Rockmusik / gern

   _____

3. du / spielen / Klavier / gut

   _____

4. Rudi und ich / kommen / aus Polen

   _____

5. wir / singen / mit dem Orchester

   _____

ÜBUNG D   **Nach dem Konzert.** You have invited your friends in the orchestra to a post-concert party. Describe who will do what using the following sentence elements.

wir	bringen	die Party
Karl	tanzen	gut
ich	hören	Spaghetti
ihr	kochen	Salat und Cola
Herr und Frau Schneider	machen	Rockmusik

EXAMPLE: **Ich mache die Party.**

1. _____

2. _____

3. _____

4. _____

5. _____

| ÜBUNG E | **Die grosse Party.** You are discussing the upcoming party with your parents and they want to know more details. Explain that Peter and Maria are coming with Lars, and that they are bringing pizza and salad. Jennifer is coming with Erich. She's bringing cola and he's bringing CDs. You will dance, listen to music and play cards. |

_____

_____

_____

_____

_____

_____

_____

3.   The Present Tense of Stem Vowel Change Verbs

Certain verbs change the vowel in the *du* and the *er/sie/es* forms before adding the endings. The verb endings remain the same. (See chart below). These verbs must be memorized.

For a complete list of commonly used strong verbs, see pages 89–96 in the appendix.

a. Verbs with stem change of *a* to *ä*

Verbs which change the stem vowel from *a* to *ä* in the *du* and *er/sie/es* forms include:

fallen, er fällt   *to fall*   **fahren, er fährt** *to drive, ride*

schlafen, er schläft *to sleep*   **tragen, er trägt**   *to wear, carry*

SINGULAR	PLURAL
ich fahre – e *I drive, I do drive, I am driving*	**wir fahr – en** *we drive, we do drive, we are driving*
du fährst – st *you (informal) drive, do drive, are driving*	**ihr fahr – t** *you (informal) drive, do drive, are driving*
er, sie, es fähr – t *he, she, or it drives, does drive, is driving*	**sie fahr – en** *they drive, they do drive, they are driving*
Sie fahr – en *you (formal) drive, do drive, are driving*	

ÜBUNG F   **Fahrweisen.** There are lots of ways and places you can drive. Create 5 different sentences from the word prompts. Can you outsmart your fellow students? See if you can create at least one sentence that no one else has.

EXAMPLE: Meine Mutter **fährt** zur Schule.

sie (they)		zur Schule
meine Mutter	→ fahren →	zu schnell
der Schüler		einen VW
ich		zum Supermarkt
du		mit Angelika

EXAMPLE: Der Schüler fährt zur Schule.

1. _____

2. _____

3. _____

4. _____

5. _____

b. Verbs with stem change of *e* to *i*

Verbs which change the stem vowel from *e* to *i* in the *du* and *er/sie/es* forms include:

essen, er isst	*to eat*	**geben, er gibt**	*to give*
helfen, er hilft	*to help*	**sprechen, er spricht**	*to speak*

SINGULAR	PLURAL
ich geb – e *I give, I do give, I am giving*	**wir geb – en** *we give, we do give, we are giving*
du gib – st *you (informal) give, do give, are giving*	**ihr geb – t** *you (informal) give, do give, are giving*
er, sie, es gib – t *he, she, or it gives, does give, is giving*	**sie geb – en** *they give, they do give, they are giving*
Sie geb – en *you (formal) give, do give, are giving*	

ÜBUNG G   **Der Stundenanfang.** Your teacher is trying to start class. You can help her by answering the following questions in complete sentences.

EXAMPLE: Wer spricht so laut?   Thomas **spricht** so laut.

1. Hilfst du am Montag oder am Dienstag? (am Dienstag)

_____

2. Wer gibt die richtige Antwort? (Jens)

_____

3. Was esst ihr auf einer Party: Salate oder Pizza? (Salate und Pizza)

_____

4. Wer spricht mit Frau Schmidt? (ich)

_____

5. Was isst du? (Nudeln)

_____

   c. Verbs with stem change of *e* to *ie*

   Verbs which change the stem vowel from *e* to *ie* in the *du* and *er/sie/es* forms include:

sehen, er sieht   *to see*   **lesen, er liest**   *to read*

SINGULAR	PLURAL
ich les – e *I read, I do read, I am reading*	**wir les – en** *we read, we do read, we are reading*
du lies – st *you (informal) read, do read, are reading*	**ihr les – t** *you (informal) read, do read, are reading*
er, sie, es lies – t *he, she, or it reads, does read, is reading*	**sie les – en** *they read, they do read, they are reading*
Sie les – en *you (formal) read, do read, are reading*	

ÜBUNG H   **Film oder Buch.** You are discussing literature and film with your teacher. For a project, you and your friends have a choice of seeing a movie or reading the book. Tell your teacher who will be doing what.

EXAMPLE: Die Braut von Frankenstein?   Anneliese **sieht** den Film.
Wilhelm Tell?   Wir **lesen** das Buch.

1. Das Phantom der Oper? (wir)

_____

2. In 80 Tagen um die Welt? (Susanna und Peter)

_____

3. Harry Potter und der Gefangene von Askaban? (Marianne)

_____

4. Der Herr der Ringe? (du)

_____

5. Einer flog über das Kuckucksnest? (mein Freund)

_____

Was geschieht hier? What are these people doing? Write a sentence for each picture.

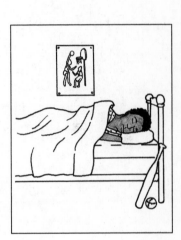

1. **Der Mann fährt ab.** _____

2. _____

3. _____

4. _____

5. _____

6. _____

ÜBUNG J   **Die Partyplanung.** Your friends are offering to help with the party you are planning for Saturday evening. Make a list of who will do what for you.

EXAMPLE: Monica/helfen/mit der Musik. Monica **hilft** mit der Musik.

1. Paul / fahren / Susi / zu der Party

   _____

2. Du / bringen / gute CDs / für die Party

   _____

3. Meine Mutter / lesen / die Gästeliste

   _____

4. Paul und Susi / sprechen / mit Frau Schneider

   _____

5. Er / essen / nicht zu viel Pizza

   _____

4.   The Present Tense of the Auxiliary Verbs *sein* and *haben*

a. The verb *sein*, like its English counterpart "to be", is strong (irregular) and changes form depending upon what or whom is being discussed.

SINGULAR		PLURAL	
ich bin	I am	**wir sind**	we are
du bist	you (informal) are	**ihr seid**	you (informal) are
er, sie, es ist	he, she, or it is	**sie sind**	they are
Sie sind you (formal) are			

ÜBUNG K   **Die Party.** At the party you must introduce your friends to your parents. Answer their questions and say something positive about everyone.

EXAMPLE: Wer ist das? (Susanne) Das ist Susanne. Sie **spielt** Klavier gut.

1. Wer ist das? (Joachim)

   _____

2. Wer sind sie? (Peter und Elke)

   _____

3. Wer ist das? (meine Freundin Antje)

   _____

4. Wer tanzt mit Brigitte? (Lars)

_____

5. Wer bringt den Salat? (die Schneiders)

_____

    b. The verb _haben_, like its English counterpart "to have", is strong (irregular) and changes form depending upon what or whom is being discussed.

SINGULAR		PLURAL	
ich habe	_I have_	**wir haben**	_we have_
du hast	_you (informal) have_	**ihr habt**	_you (informal) have_
er, sie, es hat	_he, she, or it has_	**sie haben**	_they have_
Sie haben	_you (formal) have_		

| ÜBUNG L | **Die Party.** Your friends have all brought something to the party. Using the elements involved, create sentences describing what they have when they arrive.

meine Freundin Anne ⟶ haben ⟶ eine „Tote Hose" CD
du   Pepperoni Pizza
Jessica und Andreas   zwei Freunde
ihr   Cola
Sie   Wurst und Salat

EXAMPLE: Meine Freundin Anne hat eine „Tote Hose" CD.

1. _____

2. _____

3. _____

4. _____

5. _____

5.   Separable Prefixes in the Present Tense

In English we often use a preposition to complete the meaning of a verb. We say: "I'll pick you up." or "He's driving away." In German, the completer is attached to the beginning of the verb. It starts the infinitive, yet is separated and goes to the end of its utterance (clause, phrase or sentence) when you conjugate the verb.

The most common separable prefixes and their meanings are listed in the chart below. Their meanings vary according to the root verb they are combined with, but the chart gives you a "good guess" meaning to help you decipher a verb with a separable prefix.

PREFIX	VERB	EXAMPLE	MEANING
ab *from, up*	**abfahren** *(depart, leave)* **abholen** *(pick up, fetch, get)*	**Er fährt am Freitag ab.** **Ich hole Erik ab.**	*He's leaving on Friday* *I'm picking Erik up.*
an *at, up, to*	**anrufen** *(to call up)* **ankommen** *(to arrive)*	**Wir rufen Mutter an.** **Ich komme am Montag an.**	*We are calling mother up.* *I arrive on Monday*
auf *up* **aus** *out, from*	**aufräumen** *(clean up)* **ausgehen** *(to go out)*	**Ich räume mein Zimmer auf.** **Ich gehe jetzt aus.**	*I'm cleaning up my room.* *I'm going out now.*
ein *in*	**einladen, er lädt ein** *(to invite)*	**Lädst du Jens ein?**	*Are you inviting Jens?*
mit *with, along*	**mitbringen** *(bring along, bring with)* **mitkommen** *(come with, come along)*	**Er bringt die Pizza mit.** **Mein Bruder kommt mit.**	*He's bringing the pizza with (him).* *My brother is coming along.*
vor *before*	**vorlesen** *(to read aloud, read before a group)*	**Ich lese die Namen vor.**	*I'll read the names aloud.*
nach *after*	**nachkommen** *(to follow, come later)*	**Ich komme am Dienstag nach.**	*I am coming (later) on Tuesday.*

ÜBUNG M **Die Partyplanung.** Before the party there was a lot of planning to do. Write your list of who is doing what from the following notes.

EXAMPLE: Lukas/abholen/die Pizza   Lukas **holt** die Pizza **ab**

1. Sarah / mitbringen / gute CDs

   _____

2. meine Freunde Max und Maria / abholen / Erika und Ilse

   _____

3. mein Bruder / aufräumen / das Partyzimmer

   _____

4. ich / mitbringen / Cola und Pizza

_____

5. wir / mitkommen / am Freitag

_____

| ÜBUNG N | **Wie ist die Party?** During the party a friend calls to ask how the party is going. There is a lot going on. Write who is doing what from the following notes. |

EXAMPLE: ich / tanzen / mit Lukas.   Ich **tanze** mit Lukas.

1. Jessica und Andreas / essen / Pizza

_____

2. Max / haben / viele CDs

_____

3. Suzanne / spielen / Klavier / gut

_____

4. Paul / sprechen / mit Frau Schneider

_____

5. Sarah / aufräumen / jetzt

_____

CHAPTER 2
Nouns and Articles

1. The Gender of Nouns

a. A noun is the name of a person, place or thing. Nouns in German are always capitalized.

b. In English, nouns have "natural gender". Knives, forks and spoons are neuter, i.e. they can be replaced by the pronoun "it;" a woman is "she" and a man is "he."

c. In German, nouns have grammatical gender. Every noun is assigned a gender which is unrelated to its natural gender. A spoon is masculine (*der Löffel*), a fork is feminine (*die Gabel*), and a knife is neuter (*das Messer*). The gender of a noun must be memorized along with the noun. *Der* (masculine), *die* (feminine) and *das* (neuter) are all translated in English by "the."

SOME MASCULINE NOUNS		SOME FEMININE NOUNS		SOME NEUTER NOUNS	
der Mann	*man*	**die Frau**	*woman*	**das Kind**	*child*
der Fisch	*fish*	**die Marmelade**	*jam*	**das Fleisch**	*meat*
der Saft	*juice*	**die Milch**	*milk*	**das Brot**	*bread*
der Käse	*cheese*	**die Butter**	*butter*	**das Obst**	*fruit*
der Kuchen	*cake*	**die Wurst**	*sausage*	**das Gemüse**	*vegetables*

d. There are many ways to remember the *der*, *die*, or *das* of a noun.

    1. Some students highlight or underline all the *der* words in red, the *die* words in blue, and the *das* words in green.

    2. Others enter the noun into unique *der*, *die* or *das* lists.

    3. Other students draw a mental picture of the new noun incorporating a favorite *der/die* or *das* word. We recommend a knife (*das*), fork (*die*) or spoon (*der*).

  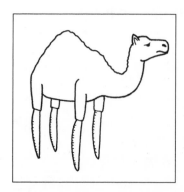

ÜBUNG A **Den Wortschatz lernen.** You have turned your mother's shopping list into a study sheet for an upcoming vocabulary test. You're experimenting with study techniques. Choose three of the words and create pictures incorporating a spoon, fork or knife in each one. You are creating a picture of the word with its gender symbol. The more outrageous your picture, the more likely you are to remember the gender of the word. Use your pictures as column head and place the rest of the words in the correct column.

Marmelade – Banane – Käse – Brot – Kuchen – Wurst – Salat – Ei – Fleisch – Kaffee – Butter - Obst

2. The Gender of a Compound Word

The gender of a compound word is always the gender of the last word in the compound.

die Mathe *math* + **das Buch** *book* = **das Mathebuch** *math book*

das Obst *fruit* + **der Kuchen** *cake* = **der Obstkuchen** *fruitcake*

ÜBUNG B **Beim Einkaufen.** You are going shopping with your mother. As she calls off the things to buy, you tell her where they are. What does she ask you? What is your answer?

EXAMPLE: Milch / dort drüben **Wo ist die Milch?** *Die Milch ist dort drüben (over there).*

1. Orangensaft / hier _____

2. Käsekuchen / dort drüben _____

3. Erdbeermarmelade / hier _____

   _____

4. Vollkornbrot / dort drüben _____

   _____

5. Zitronenbutter / dort drüben_____

   _____

3.   The Definite Article: Expressing "the"

Der, *die* and *das* are referred to as the definite article and are always translated as "the".

> **Das ist der Mathelehrer.**   *That is the math teacher.*
> **Die Kunstlehrerin heißt Frau Weibel.**   *The art teacher is called Frau Weibel.*

ÜBUNG C **Ein unvollendeter Brief.** Your friend wrote a letter and decided to play a joke on you. She left all the articles for you to fill in. Complete the letter using the correct article.

Hallo, Katrina!

D__ie__ Schule hier ist toll! D_____ Deutschlehrer Herr Bierer ist so nett. Und d_____ Deutschbuch ist interessant. D_____ Sportlehrerin ist nicht so gut. Und d_____ Mathelehrer? langweilig! Am besten finde ich d_____ Mittagspause! D_____ Käsebrot hier ist prima. Und d_____ Salat? Mmmmm . . . Dann kommt Sport. D_____ Tennisklasse ist gemischt. Wir haben 6 Jungen und 6 Mädchen. Dann? Dann ist d_____ Schultag zu Ende. Tschüs.

                                                                    Deine Franziska

ÜBUNG D **Der Zoo.** You are taking a tour of the zoo in Bern, Switzerland. You want to remember the German word and article for each animal. List them in a way that is meaningful for you: either with a picture, selective highlighting, different color inks, or in *der/die/das* lists. Your guide says:

Der Elefant dort drüben ist 12 Jahre alt und kommt aus Afrika. Die Giraffe ist erst 5 Jahre alt aber schon 2 Meter hoch. Dort drüben ist das Zebra und hinten sehen wir die neueste Antilope im Zoo. Jetzt fahren wir weiter nach Asien. Der Tiger hier vorne ist das neueste Zoobaby. Er trinkt nur Milch im Moment. Die Schlange ist aus Indien und ist 3 Meter lang. Das Krokodil hinten kommt aus Thailand und frisst Fleisch. Dort drüben ist der Braunbär, das Symbol von Bern. Wir beenden unsere Tour hier und wünschen Ihnen einen schönen Tag.

Your study sheet on the animals looks like this:

4.   Discussing People in Professions

German has different words for males and females in the same profession. To indicate that the teacher, friend, etc. is a female, add *-in* to the male form.

der Lehrer	*male teacher*	**die Lehrerin**	*female teacher*
der Pilot	*male pilot*	**die Pilotin**	*female pilot*
der Arzt	*male doctor*	**die Ärztin**	*female doctor*
der Sportler	*male athlete*	**die Sportlerin**	*female sports figure*
der Schüler	*male pupil*	**die Schülerin**	*female pupil*
der Student	*male univ. student*	**die Studentin**	*female univ. student*
der Freund	*male friend*	**die Freundin**	*female friend*
der Berater	*male advisor*	**die Beraterin**	*female advisor*
der Soldat	*male soldier*	**die Soldatin**	*female soldier*
der Polizist	*male policeman*	**die Polizistin**	*female policeman*
der Klempner	*male plumber*	**die Klempnerin**	*female plumber*
der Apotheker	*male pharmacist*	**die Apothekerin**	*female pharmacist*

ÜBUNG E   **Das Jahrbuch.** You're working on the yearbook. Everyone has dressed up as the person they hope to be in twenty years. Create captions for each picture.

Lisette Brandl

Markus Nowak

Mechthild Schroeder

Thomas Walters

Gabrielle Häuser

Stefan von der Weide

EXAMPLE: Lisette Brandl ist **Ingenieurin**.

1. _____

2. _____

3. _____

4. _____

5. _____

6. _____

5.   The Indefinite Article *Ein*

Ein, eine, and *ein* are referred to as the indefinite article and are translated as "a" or "an."

Ich bringe eine Freundin mit.   *I'm bringing a (girl)friend along.*

Der Mann ist ein Freund.   *The man is a friend.*

GENDER	DEFINITE ARTICLE (THE)	INDEFINITE ARTICLE (A/AN)
masculine	der	ein
feminine	die	eine
neuter	das	ein

NOTE: Unlike English, the indefinite article is not used when stating a person's occupation or nationality.

Der Mann ist Lehrer.   *The man is a teacher.*

Die Frau ist Professorin.   *The woman is a professor.*

Der Professor ist Amerikaner.   *The (male) professor is an American.*

ÜBUNG F | **Die Yogaklasse.** You are taking an evening adult education class in yoga. Explain who is in your class.

EXAMPLE: **Herr Schmidt / Ingenieur**   *Herr Schmidt ist Ingenieur.*
Mariana Engels / Bibliothekar   *Mariana Engels ist Bibliothekarin.*

1. Mein Vater / Erdkundelehrer _____

   Meine Mutter / Mathelehrer _____

2. Jens / Fernfahrer _____

   Petra / Kinderarzt _____

3. Gerhard Halle / Schweizer _____

   Sofia Colucci / Amerikaner _____

6.   The Possessive Adjective

Adjectives showing possession (my, mine, yours, etc.) follow the same format as *ein, eine, ein.*

Hier ist ein Glas Milch.   *Das ist mein Glas Milch!*

Dort drüben ist eine Katze. Ist das *deine* Katze?   *Ja, das ist meine Katze.*

POSSESSIVE PRONOUNS	
PRONOUN	POSSESSIVE ADJECTIVE
ich *I* **du** *you (informal)*	**mein, meine, mein** *my* **dein, deine, dein** *your*

ÜBUNG G   **Meine Familie.** You are showing pictures of your family outing. Explain what you are looking at to your friend.

EXAMPLE: **my father/my mother**   *Das sind mein Vater und meine Mutter.*

1. my aunt /an elephant

   _____

2. my brother / my girlfriend

   _____

3. my sister / a child

   _____

4. my uncle / a zebra

   _____

5. my friend / my brother / a giraffe

   _____

ÜBUNG H   **Meine Deutschklasse.** You are creating a profile of your German class. Interview five classmates and ask them what their mother and father are by profession. You may need a dictionary.

EXAMPLE: **Was ist deine Mutter?**   *Meine Mutter ist Taxifahrerin.*
              Was ist dein Vater?   *Mein Vater ist Arzt.*

1. _____

   _____

2. _____

   _____

3. _____

   _____

4. _____

   _____

5. _____

   _____

7.   Negation with *kein*

German has a single word that means "none," "not a(n)," or "not any," that word is
kein. *Kein* takes the same endings as **ein, eine, ein**.

> **Ist das ein Tiger? Nein, das ist kein Tiger. Das ist ein Löwe.**
> *No, that is not a tiger. It's a lion.*
> **Hast du eine Pizza? Nein, ich habe keine Pizza.**
> *No, I don't have a pizza. (I have no pizza.)*

ÜBUNG I	**Fotos vom Zoo.** Your friend asks you questions about your zoo pictures. Answer in the negative.

EXAMPLE: Krokodil/Alligator Ist das **ein Krokodil**? Nein, das ist **kein Krokodil**. Das ist **ein Alligator.**

1. das Nilpferd / der Elefant _____

_____

2. die Katze / das Tigerbaby _____

_____

3. die Wurst / das Käsebrot _____

_____

4. die Schlange / die Giraffe_____

_____

5. der Braunbär / der Eisbär_____

_____

NOTE: *Kein* can also mean "no," "none" or "not any" when referring to quantities.

> **Hast du Papier? Nein, ich habe kein Papier.**   *I don't have any paper.*
> **Meine Tante hat keine Katzen.**   *My aunt has no cats.*
> **Kein Schüler hat seine Hausaufgaben.**   *Not one student has his homework.*

ÜBUNG J	**Nein, ich habe keine . . .** You are going to role play a young spoiled child in a skit in German class. The babysitter wants to play some games, but you claim to have nothing to play with. Answer all her questions in the negative.

EXAMPLE: Hast du Farbstifte? **Nein, ich habe keine Farbstifte.**

1. Hast du Farben? _____

_____

2. Hast du ein Buch? _____

_____

3. Hast du eine Puppe? _____

_____

4. Hast du Karten? _____

_____

5. Hast du ein Spielauto?_____

_____

ÜBUNG K **Keine Schulsachen.** You are completely out of school supplies. Answer these
questions in the negative.

EXAMPLE: Hast du Bleistifte? Nein, ich habe **keine** Bleistifte.

1. Hast du Papier? _____

2. Hast du Kulis? _____

3. Hast du ein Lineal? _____

4. Hast du eine Schultasche? _____

5. Hast du ein Etui? _____

8.   Noun Plurals

Making a noun plural in English is easy. With very few exceptions you just add an -s.
In German, all nouns form their plurals differently. Like its gender, the plural must be
memorized with each noun. The plural has no indefinite article it's always *die*.

der Mann, die Männer	die Frau, die Frauen	das Kind, die Kinder
der Fisch, die Fische	die Milch - no plural	das Krokodil, die Krokodile
der Saft, die Säfte	die Wurst, die Würste	das Zebra, die Zebras
der Kuchen, die Kuchen	die Schlange, die Schlangen	das Brot, die Brote
der Käse - no plural	die Giraffe, die Giraffen	das Fleisch no plural
der Tiger, die Tiger	die Freundin, die Freundinnen	das Buch, die Bücher
der Löwe, die Löwen	die CD, die CDs	das Auto, die Autos
der Bär, die Bären	die Mutter, die Mütter	das Baby, die Babies
der Bruder, die Brüder	die Schwester, die Schwestern	or die Babys
der Onkel, die Onkel	die Tante, die Tanten	das Foto, die Fotos
der Vater, die Väter	die Pizza, die Pizzen or die Pizzas	
der Freund, die Freunde	die Limonade, die Limonaden	
der Salat, die Salate	die Limo, die Limo or die Limos	

NOTE: Just as with gender, the last word in a compound word is the one which is
pluralized: *das Wurstbrot, die Wurstbrote*

| ÜBUNG L | **Was bringen wir mit?** You are preparing a check list for an outing with a friend. She will suggest something to bring and you supply the amount. |

EXAMPLE: Pizza.   Wir bringen 3 **Pizzas (or Pizzen).**

1. CD (5)   _____

2. Wurst (6)   _____

3. Freund (4)   _____

4. Salat (3)   _____

5. Limo (2)   _____

9.   Patterns of Plural Nouns

There is no rule for pluralizing nouns, but there are **recurring patterns** that will help you make intelligent guesses if you have forgotten the plural of a noun. The most common are listed below.

a.   Add an *–e* (often pluralizes *der*-words and *das*-words)

der Salat, die Salate	**das Heft, die Hefte**
der Fisch, die Fische	**das Paket, die Pakete**
der Tisch, die Tische	**das Brot, die Brote**
der Bleistift, die Bleistifte	**das Schwein, die Schwein**
der Freund, die Freunde	**das Jahr, die Jahre**

b.   Add an *umlaut* **and an** *–e* (often pluralizes monosyllabic words with *a, u,* or *o*)

der Sohn, die Söhne	**die Stadt, die Städte**
der Gast, die Gäste	**die Hande, die Hände**
der Baum, die Bäume	**die Kuh, die Kühe**
der Ball, die Bälle	**die Frucht, die Früchte**

c.   Add an *–er* (often pluralizes monosyllabic *das*-words)

das Lied, die Lieder	**das Ei, die Eier**
das Kind, die Kinder	**das Kleid, die Kleider**
das Bild, die Bilder	

d. Add an *umlaut* and an *–er* (often pluralizes *der*-words and *das*-words)

der Mann, die Männer   das Land, die Länder

der Wald, die Wälder   das Haus, die Häuser

e. Add an *–n* (often pluralizes *die*-words ending in *–e, -ei, -er* or *-el*)

die Tante, die Tanten   die Schwester, die Schwestern

die Tafel, die Tafeln   die Nichte, die Nichten

die Hose, die Hosen   die Bäckerei, die Bäckereien

f. Add an *–en* (often pluralizes *die*-words ending in *–schaft, -heit, -ung, -ei* or *-keit*)

der Polizist, die Polizisten   die Freundschaft, die Freundschaften

der Student, die Studenten   die Krankheit, die Krankheiten

g. Add an *–nen* (pluralizes *die*-words ending in *–in*)

die Lehrerin, die Lehrerinnen   die Freundin, die Freundinnen

die Schülerin, die Schülerinnen   die Ärztin, die Ärztinnen

h. **No change from singular** (often pluralizes *der* / *das*-words ending in *–el* or *–er*)

der Onkel, die Onkel   der Lehrer, die Lehrer

der Tiger, die Tiger   der Enkel, die Enkel

i. Add an *umlaut* to the stressed vowel

der Garten, die Gärten   die Tochter, die Töchter

der Bruder, die Brüder   die Mutter, die Mütter

der Vater, die Väter

j. Add an *–s* (often pluralizes contemporary words of foreign origin)

der Park, die Parks   das Auto, die Autos

das Hotel, die Hotels   das Sofa, die Sofas

der Kuli, die Kulis   das Foto, die Fotos

das Baby, die Babys (or Babies)   das Hobby, die Hobbys (or Hobbies)

die Pizza, die Pizzas (or Pizzen)

10.   Definite and Indefinite Articles in the Plural

Regardless of the gender, the article for all nouns in the plural is *die*. The indefinite article for all nouns in the plural ends in *–e* (ex. *meine, deine, keine*).

SINGULAR			PLURAL
MASCULINE	FEMININE	NEUTER	
der	die	das	die
ein	eine	ein	keine

ÜBUNG M   **Mein Stammbaum.** You are working on a family tree for your journal. It need not be your own. Draw the tree on a separate sheet of paper including everyone you know within three generations. This would include grandparents, parents, children, aunts, uncles, brothers, sisters and cousins. When you are done, create a list stating how many of each relationship are on your chart. Divide your list into male and female.

EXAMPLE: **2 Brüder, 3 Onkel, 2 Großväter, . . .**

JUNGEN UND MÄNNER	MÄDCHEN UND FRAUEN

ÜBUNG N   **Die Arche Noahs.** You are making a list of things that Noah, in the story about the Ark, would take with him. You will need two of everything. Don't forget to look up the words in a dictionary to find the plural forms. After you have done the first five, use the dictionary to find four more.

EXAMPLE: der Tiger   2 **Tiger**

die Kuh   2 **Kühe**

1. der Hund   _____

2. die Katze   _____

3. das Pferd   _____

4. der Hirsch _____

5. der Eisbär _____

6. _____

7. _____

8. _____

9. _____

10. _____

ÜBUNG O   **Ein Familienfoto.** You're describing a family photo to your new friends at school. Identify at least 5 people to them and tell a little about them. Your descriptions might include their relationship to you, their age, their nationality and/or their profession.

EXAMPLE: **Der Mann dort drüben ist mein Onkel. Er ist 38 Jahre alt und Bäcker in Berlin.**

1. _____

2. _____

3. _____

4. _____

5. _____

CHAPTER 3

Subject Pronouns
Forms of Address
Imperatives

1.   Subject Pronouns

A noun is the name of a person, place or thing. A pronoun replaces a noun.

Wo ist meine Mutter? *Sie* **ist dort drüben.**

SUBJECT PLURAL			
SINGULAR		PLURAL	
ich *I*		**wir** *we*	
du *you (informal)*		**ihr** *you (informal)*	
er *he*		**sie** *they*	
sie *she*			
es *it*			
Sie *you (formal, both singular and plural)*			

2.   Using Subject Pronouns

Pronoun use is easy in English. We use "he", "she" or "it" depending upon the natural gender of the noun. In German, the grammatical gender governs which pronoun you use.

   Ich sitze am Tisch 5. Wo ist *er*?   *I'm sitting at Table 5.   Where is* it?

The pronoun *er* was used because *Tisch* (table) is a *der*-word. A *die*-word would be replaced by the pronoun *sie* and a *das*-word by the pronoun *es*.

| ÜBUNG A | **Beim Einkaufen.** Remember when you were shopping with your mother on page 13? Your answers were too long and unnatural. You wrote: „**Wo ist die Marmelade? Die Marmelade ist hier**". Return to that exercise and complete it again, this time sounding more natural. |

EXAMPLE: **Wo ist die Marmelade?**   *Sie* **ist hier.**

ÜBUNG B | **Wo sind meine Sachen?** You're getting ready to go out with your friends and can't seem to find anything. Thank goodness for your mother. She's able to tell you where everything is. What does she say? Use two sentences for each answer. Start the first sentence with *hier*.

EXAMPLE: **Wo ist mein Buch? hier / im Keller**   **Hier ist *es*. *Es* ist im Keller.**

1. Wo ist meine Kamera?   hier / im Keller

_____

2. Wo sind meine Schuhe?   hier / in deinem Zimmer

_____

3. Wo sind Batterien für die Kamera?   hier / im Schreibtisch

_____

4. Wo ist mein Volleyball?   hier / in der Garage

_____

5. Wo bist du?   hier / in der Küche.

_____

ÜBUNG C | **Du hilfst deiner Freundin.** Your friend has tried to write a short story in German, but she is not sure which German pronouns to use. Help her out by filling in the correct German pronoun.

Herr und Frau Marz wohnen in Salzburg. _____ haben einen Sohn und zwei Töchter.

Der Sohn heisst Markus. _____ ist 14 Jahre alt. Die Töchter heissen Margot und Katja. _____

sind Zwillinge und sind 12 Jahre alt. Markus hat ein Fahrrad. _____ ist ganz neu. Er hat auch

einen Helm. _____ ist rot und schwarz. Die Zwillinge haben auch Fahrräder. _____ sind blau

und fahren sehr schnell. Am Samstag fahren _____ mit Markus zum Spielplatz. _____ ist

nicht weit weg. Am Spielplatz ist eine Frau mit Luftballons. Sie . . . .

ÜBUNG D | **Das Ende der Geschichte.** While helping your friend you spill your drink on her paper. The last 4 or 5 sentences are now illegible. Finish the story for her trying to imagine what she had written.

_____

_____

_____

_____

_____

3.   Choosing the Correct Form of Address

Unlike English, German has three different words for the pronoun you: _du, ihr_ and _Sie_. The one you use depends upon your relationship to the person with whom you are speaking. The chart below will help you choose which word to use:

PRONOUN MEANING YOU	USE WHEN SPEAKING WITH.
du (singular, informal)	a close friend, a fellow student, a child, a member of your family, or an animal. You will always be on first name basis with a **du** person.
ihr (plural, informal)	two or more good friends, children, fellow students, members of the family, or animals.
Sie (singular and plural, formal)	an adult (or adults) who isn't a close friend, an adult (or adults) with whom you are not on first name basis, someone superior to you in rank or status.

NOTE: When addressing a small group with both _du_ and _Sie_ people together, it is acceptable to use _ihr_. In a large group or business setting, you would use _Sie_ when speaking to the group and continue to address individuals in the customary _du_ or _Sie_ manner.

| ÜBUNG E | **Du, ihr oder Sie?** You are meeting new people today. Circle the correct form of address that you or your conversational partner would use in each instance. |

EXAMPLE: Du bist 14 Jahre alt und sprichst mit deiner Mutter.   (du)/ ihr / Sie

1. Du bist 14 Jahre alt und sprichst mit 2 Freundinnen.   du / ihr / Sie

_____

2. Du bist 45 Jahre alt und sprichst mit dem Bäcker.   du / ihr / Sie

_____

3. Du bist 15 Jahre alt und sprichst mit deinem Lehrer.   du / ihr / Sie

_____

4. Du bist 15 Jahre alt und der Lehrer spricht mit dir.   du / ihr / Sie

_____

5. Du bist 5 Jahre alt und sprichst mit deiner 5-jährigen Cousine.   du / ihr / Sie

_____

6. Du bist 15 Jahre alt und sprichst mit deinem 5-jährigen Hund.   du / ihr / Sie

_____

7. Du bist 35 Jahre alt und sprichst mit deinen 2 Mitarbeitern.   du / ihr / Sie

_____

ÜBUNG F   **Fragen in der Schule.** You are in school for the first day and have some questions for the people you meet. Ask them using the correct form of "you." Make sure to use the correct form of the verb for the pronoun you choose. (See pp. 25, 27)

EXAMPLE: Herr Bierer / wann / English geben?
Herr Bierer, wann geben **Sie** Englisch?

1. Erika / wann / Mathe haben

_____

2. Susanna und Josef / wo / Fußball spielen

_____

3. Hannelore / wo / wohnen

_____

4. Meine Freunde / was / jetzt machen

_____

5. Frau Tedeschka / wo / herkommen

_____

4.   Giving Commands or Instructions: Imperative

When giving a command either in English or German you rarely use the word "you."

Come here. Turn at the corner. Don't stay out too late. Please help me.

In German, there are three different command forms, depending upon whether you use _du_, _ihr_, or _Sie_ with the person(s) who is to perform the action. The chart on the following page will guide you in choosing the correct form. Note that all commands are punctuated with an exclamation point.

PRONOUN MEANING YOU	COMMAND FORM

du   *(singular, informal)*
 	
Komm her! Komme her!
 	
Gib mir das Buch!
Iss dein Frühstück!
Lies das Buch!
 	
Fahr langsam!
Schlaf gut!
	(1) Use verb stem with no ending*
	       kommen = Komm her!
	(2) If the verb has an **e** *to* **i** *or* **e** *to* **ie** *vowel change in the present tense, retain the vowel change in the command.*
	       lesen = Lies das Buch!
	(3) Do **not** *change the vowel if the change is from a to ä*
	       fahren = Fahr langsam!
	*You may add an –**e** *if desired*
	       Komm her! Komme her!

ihr   *(plural, informal)*
 	
Bringt eure Bücher mit!
Esst euer Gemüse auf!
 	
Öffnet die Tür um 3 Uhr!
	(1) Use verb stem and add –**t** *to the end. Do not make any vowel changes.*
	       spielen = Spielt nicht so laut!
	(2) If the verb stem ends in –**d**, –**t**, *or two consonants followed by an* –**n**, *add* –**et** *to the end rather than a* –**t**.
	       arbeiten = Arbeitet zu zweit!

Sie *(singular and plural, formal)* **Kommen Sie morgen um 10 Uhr!**	*Use the infinitive with the pronoun* **Sie** **laufen = Laufen Sie schnell!**

NOTE: As with all verbs, if the verb has a separable prefix, the prefix is separated from the root verb in all three command forms and sent to the end of its phrase.

anfangen	**(du)**	**Fang** jetzt **an!**	*Begin now.*
	(ihr)	**Fangt** jetzt **an!**	
	(Sie)	**Fangen Sie** jetzt **an!**	

NOTE: Sein (*to be*) is an irregular verb and has the following command forms:

(du)	**Sei** ruhig!	*Be quiet.*
(ihr)	**Seid** brav!	*Be good.*
(Sie)	**Seien Sie** nicht so laut!	*Don't be so loud.*

ÜBUNG G	**Babysitten.** You are babysitting for your younger sister. You have lots of suggestions to keep her occupied. You say:

EXAMPLE: herkommen   **Komm(e) her!**

1. mit deinem Teddybär spielen _____

2. ein Buch mit mir lesen _____

3. deine Kekse essen _____

4. das Zimmer mit mir aufräumen _____

5. „die Sesamstrasse" ansehen _____

6. in die Küche gehen _____

7. schön schlafen _____

ÜBUNG H **Simon sagt . . .** You are going to play a game of "Simon Says" in your class room. Since the commands will be for the entire class you will use the *Ihr* form. Use the following words to write out your commands.

EXAMPLE: aufstehen **Steht Auf!**

1. das Buch aufmachen _____

2. das Buch schließen _____

3. den Kuli aufheben _____

4. den Kuli auf den Tisch setzen _____

5. „Guten Tag" sagen _____

6. euch setzen _____

7. mit dem Finger auf mich zeigen _____

ÜBUNG I **Bitten an die Lehrer.** You ask your teachers for help often during the day. Since the commands will be for an adult you will use the *Sie* form and because you are polite, you'll add *bitte*, which means please. Use the following words to write out your commands.

EXAMPLE den Satz wiederholen **Wiederholen Sie** den Satz **bitte!**

1. die Übung erklären _____

2. das Buch zeigen _____

3. mir einen Kuli leihen _____

4. lauter sprechen _____

5. das Wort aussprechen _____

6. auf die Tafel schreiben _____

7. dir helfen _____

ÜBUNG J   **Alltagsdeutsch in deiner Klasse.** You and your classmates are trying to write down a list of commands that the students and your German teacher normally use in class. Each of you must list three commands the teacher gives to the students both individually or as a class and two you might give to the teacher.

EXAMPLE   **Geh** bitte an die Tafel! **Geht** bitte an die Tafel!
Frau Tetzlaf, **sprechen Sie** bitte langsamer!

1. _____

2. _____

3. _____

4. _____

5. _____

ÜBUNG K   **Die Schulfestplanung.** You are responsible for an upcoming international festival at your school. You have made a list of duties and must now write appropriate notes to each person or group. Use the appropriate form of "you" when writing your instructions to each person or group of persons.

EXAMPLE: Hermann und Bettina (deine Freunde) / um 16 Uhr kommen
Kommt um 16 Uhr!

1. Madame Gautier (die Französischlehrerin) / 50 Croissants / kaufen

_____

2. Sung Li (Schülerin) / 2 chinesische Lieder / singen

_____

3. Piotr und Katarzyna (Schüler aus Polen) / Polka um 16.45 Uhr / tanzen

_____

4. Maria / 5 Pizzas / mitbringen

_____

5. Herr Garcia und Frau Lopez (die 2 Spanischlehrer) / Paella / kochen

_____

CHAPTER 4
Word Order

1. Word Order in a Declarative Statement

There are definite rules for word order in a German sentence, but there is also great flexibility. Any word or element you wish to emphasize may be placed first in a declarative statement. An element is a collection of words that must stay together in order to make sense. In the case of the sample sentence variations below, *meine Freundin* and *zur Klasse* are both elements comprised of more than one word. *Immer* and *spät* are single word elements.

You may make any word or element you wish the first element in your sentence. Usually it is the word you wish to emphasize.

Question:	**Wer kommt immer spät zur Klasse?**
Statement:	*Meine Freundin kommt immer spät zur Klasse.*
Question:	**Wann kommt deine Freundin spät zur Klasse.**
Statement:	*Immer kommt meine Freundin spät zur Klasse.*
Question:	**Wohin kommt deine Freundin immer spät?**
Statement:	*Zur Klasse kommt meine Freundin immer spät.*
Question:	**Wie kommt deine Freundin immer zur Klasse?**
Statement:	*Spät kommt meine Freundin immer zur Klasse.*

Regardless of which element is first, the verb is the second element in every declarative sentence, i.e. in every statement.

ÜBUNG A | **Ein Wettrennen.** You're having a contest with your friend. Your teacher has given you seven sentence elements and asked you to construct as many different sentences as possible from them. You are racing with your friend to see who can be the first to create 5 different sentences. You write:

um acht Uhr / am Samstag / mit meiner Schwester / endlich / zur Schule / ich / fahren

EXAMPLE   Mit meiner Schwester fahre ich endlich um acht Uhr am Samstag zur Schule.

1. _____

2. _____

3. _____

4. _____

5. _____

ÜBUNG B   **Der erste Schultag.** Your younger brother is excited about his first day of school. He keeps asking you the same questions over and over again and you are losing your patience. You show your impatience by raising your tone of voice and placing the information he wants first in the sentence.

EXAMPLE: Wann beginnt meine Schule? / um 8.15   **Um 8.15** beginnt deine Schule.

1. Wer ist mein Lehrer? / Herr Rohrbach

   _____

2. Wann fahren wir ab? / in zehn Minuten

   _____

3. Was bringe ich mit? / ein Buch und dein Brotpaket

   _____

4. Wer ist in meiner Klasse? / Katarina und Rita

   _____

5. Wie fahre ich zur Schule? / mit dem Schulbus

   _____

ÜBUNG C   **Dein Schultag.** Your German speaking pen pal has emailed you a list of questions about your school and your school day. Use the elements listed below to write a return message. Answer her sentences by always starting the sentences with the first element given. Put the rest of the elements in the correct order. Do not forget that the verb is the second element in every declarative sentence.

EXAMPLE: Um 7.50 Uhr / die Schule / beginnen
          Um 7.50 Uhr **beginnt** mein Schultag.

1. um 8.40 Uhr / Mathe / ich / haben

   _____

2. in Mathe / viel / wir / lernen

   _____

3. abends / viele Mathehausaufgaben / wir / haben

   _____

4. in der Schule /viel Spass / wir / haben

   _____

5. nach der Schule / Sport / wir / spielen

   _____

2.   Word Order in an Interrogative Sentence

Just as in English, there are two ways to ask a question in German: with or without a question word.

a. Forming a Question with an Interrogative

There are seven major interrogatives, or question words, in German:

QUESTION WORDS (INTERROGATIVES) IN GERMAN	
wer *who*	**wie** *how*
was *what*	**warum** *why*
wo (woher, wohin) *where (from where, where to)*	**wieviel (wie viele)** *how much (how many)*
wann *when*	

When using an interrogative to form a question, the interrogative is the first element in the sentence, followed by the verb.

Wann isst du dein Frühstück?   *When do you eat your breakfast?*

Was höre ich jetzt zu?   *What am I listening to now?*

ÜBUNG D   **Fragen?** You are playing a game with your German speaking friends. The goal is to ask the question for the answers that you read. Write the question that most likely fits the answers below.

EXAMPLE: Um 8.15 beginnt meine Schule. **Wann** beginnt deine Schule?

1. Das ist Michael._____

2. Helmut wohnt in Giessen. _____

3. Er kommt um 7.45 Uhr._____

4. Er bringt seine Videospiele mit._____

5. Er hat sieben Spiele._____

b. Forming a Question when there is no Interrogative

You may also create a question without using an interrogative. Just as in English, inverting the verb and making it the first element in the sentence turns any statement into a question.

Statement: **Du bringst die Pizzas.**   *You are bringing the pizzas.*

Question: **Bringst du die Pizzas?**   *Are you bringing the pizzas?*

ÜBUNG E	**Ein Tag im Park.** You are planning a day in the park with your friends. Make a list of questions for your friends using the notes below.

EXAMPLE. wir / gehen / um Mittag   Gehen wir um Mittag?

1. Herbert / bringen / den Fussball

   _____

2. Jessie / kommen / auch

   _____

3. wir / spielen / bis 3.00 Uhr

   _____

4. wir / gehen / ins Restaurant

   _____

5. wir / sein / um 8.00 Uhr / zu Hause

   _____

3. The Order of Modifiers in a Sentence

a. Modifiers, either individual words or elements, fall into one of three categories: time (when), manner (how) and place (where, where to, or where from). There is no specific position in the sentence for modifiers. In the sample below, we wanted to emphasize the fact that the girl is drinking her milk quickly, so that she can return to the playroom. Quickly (*schnell*) then became the first element. As long as the verb is the second element in a statement, any word may become the first element, including a modifier.

> **Schnell trinkt sie ihre Milch und geht zurück zum Spielraum.**
> *She drinks her milk quickly and goes back to the playroom.*

b. Modifiers need not be positioned together, but they should appear in the sentence in the order of TMP: time (when) - manner (how) - and place (where). This is tricky since it is the opposite in English. We usually mention the place first and then the time. He's coming home tomorrow. In German the preferred word order is: **Er kommt morgen nach Hause.**

c. The only exception to the TMP rule is: any modifier you wish to emphasize may be brought forward in the sentence to the first position. It is then followed by the verb and then any remaining modifiers in the order time-manner-place.

> **Morgen geht sie mit Maria zur Schule.**
> TMP: Time = **morgen**, manner = **mit Maria**, and place = **zur Schule**

| ÜBUNG F | **Ein Brief über deinen Tag im Park.** You are writing a letter to your German-speaking relative in Austria. Use the elements below to write your relative about what you plan to do on your day in the park. There are many correct ways to write these sentences. Remember the rules explained above. |

EXAMPLE: um Mittag/in den Park/wir/gehen   Wir gehen um Mittag in den Park.

1. lang und hart / wir / spielen

   _____

2. zum Park / später / Jessie / kommen

   _____

3. zum Restaurant / um 3.00 Uhr / Jessie und ich / gehen

   _____

4. nach Hause / um 5.00 Uhr / mit dem Bus / fahren

   _____

5. mit der Familie / um 7.00 Uhr / zu Hause / essen

   _____

| ÜBUNG G | **Ein Brief über deine Familie.** You have invited an Austrian student to your home for two weeks this summer. Write him a letter in German telling him about your family and what you do in your town in the summer. Make your letter as interesting as possible by introducing several modifiers and varying the word order. |

_____

_____

_____

_____

_____

_____

CHAPTER 5
Adjectives and Adverbs

1. Ein-words (*ein, mein, dein, kein*)

You've already learned that nouns have a gender; i.e., they are either masculine (*der*), feminine (*die*), or neuter (*das*). When preceded by an *ein*-word (*ein, dein, mein,* or *kein*), that *ein*-word also takes a unique ending.

Singular	der Rock	⟶	ein, mein, dein or kein Rock
	die Bluse	⟶	eine, meine, deine or keine Bluse
	das Kleid	⟶	ein, mein, dein, or kein Kleid
Plural	die Röcke, Blusen, Kleider	⟶	meine, deine or keine Röcke, Blusen, Kleider

---

ÜBUNG A   **Ist das eine . . . ?** Your friend is learning German. You are playing a game and when you point at something you say the German word and your friend must answer in a sentence using **ein,** or **eine.**

EXAMPLE: Die Bluse   Ja, das ist **eine** Bluse.

1. der Rock

_____

2. die Jacke

_____

3. das Hemd

_____

4. der Schuh

_____

5. der Mantel

_____

2. Possessive Adjectives

Just as in English, each pronoun has its unique possessive form. When "he" owns something, it is "his." If "we" own it, it is "ours." The chart on the following page lists all the possessive pronouns in German. They are all *ein*-words and take the same endings as *ein, mein, dein* and *kein.*

POSSESSIVE ADJECTIVES			
SINGULAR		PLURAL	
PRONOUN	POSSESSIVE ADJECTIVE	PRONOUN	POSSESSIVE ADJECTIVE
ich	mein, meine, mein *my*	wir	unser, *unsere our*
du	dein, deine, dein *your*	ihr	euer, *euere, euer your*
er	sein, seine, sein *his*	sie	ihr, ihre, ihr *their*
sie	ihr, ihre, ihr *her*		
es	sein, seine, sein *its*		
Sie	Ihr, Ihre, Ihr *your*		

NOTE: *The middle *e* is optional when adding endings to *unser* or *euer*. You may use *unsere* or *unsre* / *euere* or *eure*.

ÜBUNG B   **Wessen?** (Whose?) You are cleaning up after a camping trip. Use an appropriate possessive adjective to identify what belongs to whom.

EXAMPLE: die Jacke / Heike   Das ist **ihre** Jacke.   That is **her** Jacket.

1. der Mantel / Max

   _____

2. die Hose / Manuela

   _____

3. das Hemd / Herr Schmidt

   _____

4. der Rock / Anja

   _____

5. der Regenschirm / Teddy und Theo

   _____

ÜBUNG C   **Das Fundbüro.** (Lost and found) Now that you know what belongs to him, call to the people and tell them where their lost article is. Use the same list as above. Assume that you are on "*du* terms" with all those identified by their first names.

EXAMPLE: die Jacke / Heike   Heike, hier ist **deine** Jacke.

1. _____
2. _____
3. _____
4. _____
5. _____

3. Matching the Correct Possessive to a Noun

Assigning the correct possessive to a noun is not as easy in German as in English. English has natural gender. The skirt's length is "its" length. The blouse's collar is "its" collar. In German, choosing the correct possessive is a two-step procedure. You must first determine the gender of the noun to which the possessive refers.

der Rock (skirt) is masculine.   The possessive is **sein** (his).

die Bluse (blouse) is feminine.   The possessive is **ihr** (hers).

das Kleid (dress) is neuter.   The possessive is **sein** (its).

When discussing the skirt's length in German, you say "his" length, because *der Rock* is a masculine noun. The blouse's collar is "her" collar because *die Bluse* is a feminine noun. Even though we translate the word as "its," the German possessive is *sein* (his), *ihr* (hers) or *sein* (its) depending upon the gender of the word the possessive refers to.

Das ist mein Rock.   **Seine** Länge ist perfekt.   *Its length is perfect.*

Ist das deine Bluse?   Ihr **Kragen ist sehr hübsch.**   *Its collar is very pretty.*

Look at the examples above closely. It's important to remember that the choice of which possessive to use (*mein, dein, sein, ihr, unser, euer,* or *Ihr*) is dependent upon the noun it refers to. If it's a person, it's just like in English. If I own it, it's *mein.* If he owns it, it's *sein* (his). If you're referring to a Krawatte (for example, the tie's polka dots), then it's *ihre Punkte* (her polka dots) because the tie is a feminine noun.

When you've chosen the proper word then you look at the noun it modifies to see whether you use *sein, seine,* or *sein.*

ÜBUNG D   **Meine Kleidung.** You are writing an e-mail to your friend about your new wardrobe. Describe the good things about your new clothing using the words given below. Remember: The grammatical gender determines which possessive you use and the following noun determines the ending.

EXAMPLE: die Jacke - _____Ihre_____ Farbe ist wunderbar!

1. der Mantel - _____ Länge ist perfekt.

2. die Hose - _____ Stoff ist sehr warm.

3. das Hemd - _____ Kragen ist sehr breit.

4. der Rock - _____ Muster ist sehr farbig.

5. der Pulli - _____ Stoff ist leicht.

6. der Hut - _____ Farbe finde ich gut.

7. die Bluse - _____ Muster ist schön.

| ÜBUNG E | **Wessen Kleidung?** You are helping your mother separate your clothing from Lars', your cousin who is visiting. As she picks up the article and says its name, you answer by saying whether it is yours or his.

EXAMPLE: **das Hemd**   Das ist **mein** Hemd.
die Schuhe (Lars)   Das sind **seine** Schuhe.

1. der Mantel (Lars)

   _____

2. das T-Shirt

   _____

3. die Socken (Lars)

   _____

4. die Shorts

   _____

5. der Hut (Lars)

   _____

6. das Hemd

   _____

7. die Hose (Lars)

   _____

8. die Mütze

   _____

9. die Lederjacke (Lars)

   _____

10. die Sommerjacke

    _____

11. der Pulli

    _____

ÜBUNG F | **Danke für die Kleidung.** You are helping your cousin write a thank you note for clothing he received from relatives during his trip to Austria. He is not sure how to use possessive adjectives so you fill in the blanks for him.

Liebe Tante Gerda,

ich habe meine neuen Kleider sehr gern. Das Hemd ist schön. _____Seine_____ Farbe ist perfekt. Die Jacke ist auch wunderbar. _____ Kragen ist breit. Ich mag die Hose. _____ Länge ist genau richtig. Die Socken sind prima. _____ Punkte sind so lustig! Und ich liebe die Schuhe. Ich mag _____ Farbe sehr. Vielen Dank für alles.

Liebe Grüße

Dein Volker

4.   Adjectives

An adjective describes (modifies) a person, place or thing. Colors, for example, are often used as an adjective to describe a noun. Stand alone adjectives that *follow a linking* verb need no endings.

Ihr Mantel ist blau. Seine Krawatte ist gestreift. Sein Hemd ist weiß. Unsere Schuhe sind braun. Mein Rock ist lang.

ÜBUNG G | **Die Lehrerin trägt . . .** You are describing what your teacher, Frau Humboldt, is wearing today. Add an adjective to each of the sentences.

EXAMPLE: Bluse / hübsch   **Ihre** Bluse ist hübsch.

1. Rock _____

2. Schuhe _____

3. Halskette _____

4. Handtasche _____

5. Mantel _____

6. Schal _____

7. Bluse _____

8. Armbanduhr _____

5. Adverbs

An adverb modifies a verb, an adjective or another adverb. It usually answers the question "when," "how", "how much," or "to what extent." Adverbs take no endings in German.

Ich backe <u>oft</u>. Meine Schokoladentorte ist <u>super</u> gut. Ich backe sie <u>sehr</u> langsam.

ÜBUNG H   **Unsere Fußballmannschaft.** You are going to tell the class about you soccer team. Use the following to write some notes.

EXAMPLE: wir / spielen / oft   Wir spielen **oft.**

1. wir / spielen / gut

   _____

2. manchmal / gewinnen / das Team

   _____

3. Rudi / spielen / besonders / hart

   _____

4. Unser Trainer / schreien / sehr / laut

   _____

5. Unsre Mannschaft / sein /echt/gut

   _____

ÜBUNG J   **Die Klassensprecherin.** Your friend has asked you to write a letter of recommendation for her. She's running for **Klassensprecherin**. Try and vary your sentence structure while letting the people know that your friend is: **ehrlich, 100% verantwortungsvoll, dynamisch, intelligent, super hilfsbereit, besonders freundlich, und klug.**

Meine Freundin . . .

_____

_____

_____

_____

_____

_____

_____

CHAPTER 6
The Direct Object

1.   The Direct Object

A direct object tells who or what receives the action of the verb.

Ich trage eine Bluse.   *I'm wearing a blouse.*
Sie hat eine Schwester und einen Bruder.   *She has a sister and a brother.*

a. Forms of the direct object

The endings for the direct object are the same as for the nominative except in the masculine singular.*

	MASCULINE	FEMININE	NEUTER	PLURAL
nominative	**der**	**die**	**das**	**die**
accusative	**den***	**die**	**das**	**die**

	MASCULINE	FEMININE	NEUTER	PLURAL
nominative	**ein**	**eine**	**ein**	**meine**
accusative	**einen***	**eine**	**ein**	**meine**

ÜBUNG A **Ein Klassenspiel.** You are making up a game for your German class. You will hold up pictures and your classmates will respond by saying, "I see the _____." Create the answer key using the word prompts below.

EXAMPLE: das Buch   Ich sehe **das** Buch.

1. der Bleistift_____

2. die Frau _____

3. der Mann _____

4. der Kuli _____

5. das Etui _____

6. die Kreide _____

7. das Heft _____

8. die Mappe _____

9. die Tafel _____

10. die Uhr _____

ÜBUNG B   **Noch ein Klassenspiel.** For the second game, you will show the picture and ask, "Do you see the _____?" The students will respond, "Yes, I see a _____." Once again, write out the answer key using the word prompts below.

EXAMPLE: Siehst du **den** Bleistift?   Ja, ich sehe **einen** Bleistift.

1. Siehst du das Buch? _____

2. Siehst du die Kreide? _____

3. Siehst du den Kuli? _____

4. Siehst du die Frau? _____

5. Siehst du das Kind? _____

6. Siehst du die Uhr? _____

7. Siehst du das Heft? _____

8. Siehst du den Mann? _____

ÜBUNG C   **Mein Mittagessen.** Your friends are trying to find out what you have for lunch. You've asked them to guess. Respond to their guesses according to the samples below.

EXAMPLE: Nudelsalat /nein   Nein, ich habe **keinen** Nudelsalat.
           Banane / ja   Ja, ich habe **eine** Banane.

1. Käsebrot / ja _____

2. Limo / nein _____

3. 2 Kekse / nein _____

4. Eistee / ja _____

5. Apfel / ja _____

| ÜBUNG D |

Eine Übung aus der Schweiz. Your Swiss key pal has sent you an exercise to help you learn the direct object forms of the definite and indefinite articles. Fill in the endings.

Remember: *ein, dein, mein,* and *kein* all take the same endings.

EXAMPLE: Heute kaufe ich ein___ **en** ___ Wintermantel.

1. Ich kaufe auch ein_____ Pulli.

2. Connie kauft ein_____ Jacke und ein_____ Mantel.

3. Ich mag ihr_____ Mantel.

4. Der Mantel hat nur ein_____ Tasche.

5. Sie trägt ein_____ Bluse, ein_____ Rock und ein_____ Gürtel.

2.   Direct Object Pronouns

When replacing a noun with a pronoun, you must make sure that it has the same gender (masculine, feminine or neuter), the same number (singular or plural) and the same case (nominative or accusative) as the noun it replaces. You already know the pronouns *ich* (I), *du* (you), *er, sie* and *es* (he, she, and it), *wir* (we), *ihr* (you plural), *sie* (they), and *Sie* (formal you). The following chart gives you the accusative (direct object) form of those pronouns.

DIRECT OBJECT PRONOUNS	
SINGULAR	PLURAL
mich *me* **dich** *you (informal)*	**uns** *us* **euch** *you (informal)*
ihn *him* **sie** *her* **es** *it*	**sie** *them*
Sie *you (formal, both singular and plural)*	

| ÜBUNG D |

Ein Familienfoto. You are discussing a picture of your family with your mother. She is asking you if you see certain people. Answer in the positive, and tell her where you see them. Use *vorne, hinten, links, rechts* und *in der Mitte* when describing their positions.

EXAMPLE: Siehst du deinen Grossvater?   Ja, ich sehe **ihn vorne in der Mitte.**

1. Siehst du deine Tante Emma?

   _____

2. Siehst du deine Kusine Nadine?

   _____

3. Siehst du mich?

   _____

4. Siehst du deinen Vater?

   _____

5. Siehst du meinen Hund Micki?

   _____

NOTE: A pronoun agrees with the word it replaces in gender, number and case (GNC). In the examples below, _ihn_ is used referring to the skirt because skirt is masculine. The German says I have "him", not "it". _Sie_ (her) is used to refer to the cake because it's a feminine noun.

> Ich habe **einen Rock,** aber ich finde ihn nicht.
> _I have a skirt, but can't find it._

> Mein Bruder bäckt **die Torte,** aber ich esse **sie.**
> _My brother is baking the cake, but I will eat it._

ÜBUNG E | **Hast du alles?** You are getting ready for school and you mother wants you to prove that you have everything for class.
Answer her questions using direct object pronouns.

EXAMPLE: Hast du deinen Kuli?   Ja, Ich habe **ihn.**

1. Hast du dein Deutschbuch? _____

2. Hast du deine Mappe? _____

3. Hast du dein Heft? _____

4. Hast du deinen Bleistift? _____

5. Hast du dein Pausenbrot? _____

6. Hast du deinen Kuli? _____

7. Hast du dein Etui? _____

ÜBUNG F | **Was magst du gern?** You are visiting a family in Genf, Switzerland. The host mother is going shopping and asking you what you like to eat. Answer the questions using direct object pronouns.

EXAMPLE: Magst du Pizza?   Ja, ich mag **sie.** or Nein, ich mag **sie** nicht.

1. Magst du Käse? _____

2. Magst du Suppe? _____

3. Magst du Brot? _____

4. Magst du Fisch? _____

5. Magst du Orangensaft? _____

6. Magst du Äpfel? _____

7. Magst du Milch? _____

ÜBUNG G | **Unser Schultag.** You and your classmates are writing a story about your school day. Your partner is not sure of which direct object pronouns to use so you must complete the story below using the correct pronouns.

EXAMPLE: Der Lehrer heisst Petzhold. Ich mag___ihn___ .

Unser Lehrer ist nett und hat _____ gern. Das Klassenzimmer ist klein. Ich

finde _____ schön. Es gibt zwanzig Schüler. Ich sehe _____ jeden Tag.

Michaela ist meine Freundin. Sie hat _____ gern. Ich finde _____ perfekt.

Wir hassen die Schule nicht, wir finden _____ so-so. Michaela hat eine schwere

Schultasche. Sie trägt _____ oft.

| ÜBUNG H | **Deine Geburtstagsgeschenke.** Your key pal in Germany has asked you to write about the presents you received for your last birthday. Write him an e-mail using the format below. Tell him about 5 different presents you received. |

EXAMPLE: Ich habe ein Fahrrad bekommen. Ich mag **es**.
　　　　　Ich habe einen Pulli bekommen. Ich finde **ihn** nicht sehr schön.

_____

_____

_____

_____

_____

CHAPTER 7
Modal Helping Verbs
The Helping Verb *möchten*

There is a certain class of helping verb that allows you to express ability, permission, desire and obligation or necessity. These verbs are called modal verbs.

Ich muss zur Schule gehen.	*I have to go to school.*
Er will uns sehen.	*He wants to see us.*
Kannst du mit uns kommen?	*Can you come with us?*

1. Formation of the Present Tense

Modal verbs take the same forms as other verbs with two exceptions: there is often a vowel change in the singular, and the first and third persons (I and he/she/it) take no endings.

	DÜRFEN to be permitted to, allowed to, may	KÖNNEN to be able to, can	MÖGEN to like to, like	MÜSSEN to have to, must	SOLLEN to be supposed to, should	WOLLEN to want to, want
ich	darf	kann	mag	muss	soll	will
du	darfst	kannst	magst	musst	sollst	willst
er, sie, es	darf	kann	mag	muss	soll	will
wir	dürfen	können	mögen	müssen	sollen	wollen
ihr	dürft	könnt	mögt	müsst	sollt	wollt
sie	dürfen	können	mögen	müssen	sollen	wollen
Sie	dürfen	können	mögen	müssen	sollen	wollen

Modal verbs are used as helping verbs. Look at the sentences above and below. You will see that the modal is the second element, like all other verbs you've learned. An infinitive is placed at the end of the clause or the sentence to complete the thought of the modal.

Was kannst du mitbringen?	**Ich kann die Pizza und die Colas mitbringen.**
Wann sollen wir kommen?	**Wir sollen um acht Uhr kommen.**

> **ÜBUNG A** **Campen oder nicht campen.** You want to go to a sleep away camp this summer, but your parents aren't willing to say yes yet. Your mother is on the phone interviewing the owner of the camp to get more details. You only hear one side of the conversation. How do you think the owner is answering her questions?

EXAMPLE: Kann er jeden Tag schwimmen?   Ja, er **kann** jeden Tag **schwimmen**.

1. Müssen die Camper in Zelten schlafen?

   _____

2. Soll er einen Schlafsack haben?

   _____

3. Darf er seinen Hund mitbringen?

   _____

4. Wollen Sie seine Schulzeugnisse sehen?

   _____

5. Kann ich ihn manchmal besuchen?

   _____

NOTE: You may omit the infinitive if the meaning is clear without it.

> **Ich darf nicht.**   *I'm not allowed (to do that).*
>
> **Ihr müsst jetzt in die Stadt.**   *You have (to go) into the city now.*

2.   Word Order with Modal Verbs

The modal replaces the verb as second element (in a statement) or first element (in a question.) The infinitive completer is placed at the end of the clause.

> **Mein Vater kann uns zur Party fahren.**   *My father can drive us to the party.*
>
> **Willst du jetzt essen?**   *Do you want to eat now?*

> **ÜBUNG B** **Die Schulregeln.** Make a list of rules and regulations for your school. Use the word elements below. Since you are sending this list to your cousin in Germany and these rules apply to everyone, use *wir*.

EXAMPLE: Unsere Hausaufgaben / machen / sollen
Wir **sollen** unsere Hausaufgaben **machen**.

1. unsere Schulsachen / mitbringen / müssen

   _____

2. mit einem Kuli / schreiben / sollen

   _____

3. nur Deutsch / sprechen / dürfen

   _____

4. manchmal / an die Tafel / schreiben / müssen

_____

5. oft / ruhig / sein / sollen

_____

ÜBUNG C | **Schilder in Deutschland.** In preparation for a trip to Germany you and your classmates are looking at signs you may encounter. Fill in the blanks to demonstrate that you understand the meaning of the signs below.

EXAMPLE: hier /nicht rauchen
          Hier **darfst** du nicht **rauchen**

1. hier / Fahrrad / fahren

_____

2. hier / parken

_____

3. hier / über die Strasse / gehen

_____

4. hier / Brot / kaufen

_____

ÜBUNG D | **Deine Talente.** Was kannst du machen? Was kannst du nicht machen? Write out questions for your classmate based on the word elements below.

EXAMPLE: Deutsch sprechen   **Kannst** du Deutsch **sprechen**?

1. gut schreiben _____

2. Spanisch sprechen _____

3. Fussball spielen_____

4. Tennis spielen _____

5. schnell lesen _____

6. gut singen _____

7. ein Instrument spielen_____

| ÜBUNG E | **Fragen über deine Talente.** Now answer the questions you asked in Übung D, so that you know what to tell your classmate. |

EXAMPLE: Kannst du Deutsch sprechen?   Ja, **ich kann** Deutsch sprechen.

1. _____

2. _____

3. _____

4. _____

5. _____

6. _____

7. _____

| ÜBUNG F | **Peters Probleme. Was soll Peter machen?** You are playing a game in which your partner tells you what Peter's problem is, and you must say what he should do. Do the following exercise to get ready for the game. |

EXAMPLE: Peter hat Hausaufgaben.   Er **soll** die Hausaufgaben **machen.**

1. Er hat Hunger. _____

2. Er hat Durst. _____

3. Er ist müde. _____

4. Er hat Schule. _____

5. Er hat eine Klassenarbeit. _____

| ÜBUNG G | **Hausarbeit.** Your cousins are coming to visit you. They live in Gießen, Germany. You want to know which chores they must do at home so you prepare a list of questions using the words below. |

EXAMPLE: den Tisch decken   **Müsst** ihr den Tisch **decken?**

1. das Bett machen _____

2. das Geschirr spülen _____

3. die Blumen gießen _____

4. den Rasen mähen _____

ÜBUNG H | **Cornelias Hausarbeit.** Imagine that your cousin, Cornelia answers all of the questions above with "yes." Write what you would tell your friends Cornelia must do.

EXAMPLE: den Tisch decken   Sie **muss** den Tisch **decken**.

1. das Bett machen _____

2. das Geschirr spülen _____

3. die Blumen gießen _____

4. den Rasen mähen _____

ÜBUNG I | **Fernsehprogramme.** Make a list of five questions you can ask your German class to find out which television shows they like.

EXAMPLE: **Mögt** Ihr die <u>Simpsons</u>?

1. _____

2. _____

3. _____

4. _____

3. The Helping Verb *möchten*

The verb *möchten* translates into English as "would like."

Möchten Sie mit uns gehen?   *Would you like to go with us?*
Was möchtest du trinken?   *What would you like to drink?*

PRESENT TENSE OF **MÖCHTEN**	
SINGULAR	PLURAL
ich möcht – e *I would like*	**wir möcht – en** *we would like*
du möcht – est *you (informal) would like*	**ihr möcht – et** *you (informal) would like*
er, sie, es möcht – e *he, she, or it would like*	**sie möcht – en** *they would like*
Sie möcht – en *You (formal) would like*	

ÜBUNG J | **Tanjas Besuch.** Tanja, an exchange student from Austria, is coming to visit. You are planning activities for Saturday. You need to call her and ask her what she would like to do. Before calling you make a list of questions using the correct form of *möchten*.

EXAMPLE: in die Stadt gehen   **Möchtest** du in die Stadt **gehen**?

1. ins Restaurant gehen _____

2. ins Museum gehen _____

3. Fußball spielen _____

4. Fahrrad fahren _____

ÜBUNG K | **Was du tun sollst.** Write your pen pal a message in which you explain your duties/chores at home. You should try to tell your pen pal what you are supposed to do AND what you actually do.

List at least five chores.

EXAMPLE: Ich **soll** montags den Tisch **decken**. Aber ich vergesse oft.

_____

_____

_____

_____

_____

_____

_____

_____

CHAPTER 8

The Indirect Object
Dative Verbs
Idioms Using the Dative
Expressing Likes and Dislikes

1. The Indirect Object

The indirect object states "to whom" or "for whom" something is done.

Die Lehrerin gibt uns zu viele Hausaufgaben.	*The teacher gives us too much homework.*
Ich schenke meiner Mutter ein Buch.	*I'm giving my mother a book.*
Zeigen Sie mir bitte den Heimweg!	*Please show me the way home.*

The indirect object is always in the dative case.

2. The Dative Definite Article

The dative definite article changes form depending upon whether it is used before a masculine, feminine, neuter or plural noun.

Wir erzählen dem Rektor keine Lüge.	*We aren't telling the principal a lie.*
Ich zeige der Frau meine neue Uhr.	*I'm showing the lady my new watch.*
Die Mutter liest dem Kind ein Buch vor.	*The mother reads the child a book.*
Ich gebe den Katzen Milch.	*I am giving the cats milk.*

The following chart shows the definite articles in the dative, as well as in the nominative and accusative you already know.

THE DEFINITE ARTICLES				
	MASCULINE	FEMININE	NEUTER	PLURAL
NOMINATIVE	der	die	das	die
DATIVE	dem	der	dem	den
ACCUSATIVE	den	die	das	die

3. The Indefinite Article in the Dative Case

The chart on the following page shows the indefinite articles in the dative, as well as in the nominative and accusative you already know.

THE INDEFINITE ARTICLES			
	MASCULINE	FEMININE	NEUTER
NOMINATIVE	ein	eine	ein
DATIVE	einem	einer	einem
ACCUSATIVE	einen	eine	ein

NOTE: *Kein* and the possessive adjectives (*mein, dein, sein*) always follow the same pattern as the indefinite article.

ÜBUNG A | **Was schickst du wem?** You have several items which you must send to friends and relatives. Match a relative with an item and write a correct sentence.

EXAMPLE: Ich schicke **meinem** Onkel eine Postkarte.

mein Onkel	eine Postkarte
meine Schwester	ein Buch
meine Mutter	eine Geburtstagskarte
mein Bruder	eine CD
deine Eltern	eine Pflanze

1. _____

2. _____

3. _____

4. _____

5. _____

ÜBUNG B | **Geburtstagsgeschenke.** You have several birthdays to celebrate this month and don't want to duplicate any gifts. Your friends are discussing who's giving whom what and you've been asked to take notes.

EXAMPLE: Susanna / schenken / ihr Bruder / eine Hose
Susanna schenkt **ihrem** Bruder eine Hose.

1. ich / schenken / meine Schwester / eine CD

_____

2. wir / schenken / unser Klassenlehrer / einen Kuli

_____

3. die Kinder in der dritten Klasse / kaufen / die Lehrerin / einen Pullover

_____

4. Jens und Julia / geben / ihr Bruder / ein Fahrrad

_____

5. ich / kaufen / meine Oma und mein Opa / eine Pflanze

_____

4. Plural Nouns in the Dative

When you are using a noun in the dative plural, add an *–n* or an *–en* to the end of it. Do not add the *–n* (*-en*) if the noun already ends in *–n* or *–s*. This is one of the very few times where nouns change in German.

Onkel Klaus schenkt den Kindern immer Bonbons.

Uncle Klaus always gives the children candy.

| ÜBUNG C | **Sein neues Fahrrad.** Your younger brother got a new bicycle for his birthday. He is telling you to whom he wants to show it. |

EXAMPLE: meine Mitschüler   Ich zeige **meinen Mitschülern** mein Fahrrad.

1. meine Lehrer

   _____

2. meine Freunde

   _____

3. die Kinder

   _____

4. meine Lehrerinnen

   _____

5. unsre Eltern

   _____

5. Indirect Pronoun Objects

Just as in English, the pronoun changes when it is the dative case.

DATIVE CASE PRONOUNS	
SINGULAR	PLURAL
mir *me, to me, for me*	**uns** *us, to us, for us*
dir *you, to you, for you (informal)*	**euch** *you, to you, for you (informal)*
ihm *him, to him, for him*	
ihr *her, to her ,for her*	**ihnen** *them, to them, for them*
ihm *it, to it ,for it*	
Ihnen *you, to you, for you (formal)*	

ÜBUNG D | **Dein Schulzeugnis.** Your younger brother is causing problems again. You got a bad report card. He found it and is threatening to show it to lots of people. You question his choice of people using noun and then for emphasis, the pronoun. Note that your first sentence fragment is in the dative because you are implying "to" in your statement. (*to mother?*)

EXAMPLE: Mutter   **Der** Mutter?   Du zeigst es **ihr?**   Warum?
          dein Freund Josef   **Meinem** Freund Josef?   Du zeigst es **ihm?**   Warum?

1. deine Freundin Elena

   _____

2. deine Eltern

   _____

3. dein Kunstlehrer

   _____

4. Frau Fittighoff

   _____

5. der Fussballtrainer

   _____

6.   Word Order When Using the Indirect Object

German word order is the same as in English. If both direct and indirect object are stated as nouns, the indirect object is in front of the direct object.

Die Mutter liest ihren Kindern eine Geschichte vor.
The mother is reading her children a story.

Der Lehrer gibt seinen Schülern immer eine Pause vor Mathe.
The teacher always gives his students a break before Math.

ÜBUNG E | **Versteckspiel.** (Hide and Seek) Your pesty little brother is at it again. Your guests are ready to go home and it seems he's hidden their stuff. Ask him politely to please give it back to them. Remember that the indirect object is in the dative and the direct object in the accusative.

EXAMPLE: sein Mantel / dein Freund Robert
          Gib **meinem** Freund Robert **seinen** Mantel bitte!

1. meine Freundin Cornelia / ihre Jacke

   _____

2. die Zwillinge Thom und Sven / ihre Tennisbälle

_____

3. der Trainer / seine Teamliste

_____

4. die Westmeier Brüder / ihre Jacken

_____

5. du / dein Mathebuch

_____

If the direct object is a pronoun, the direct object precedes the indirect object.

> **Wer hat mein Buch? Gib es mir jetzt!**   *Who has my book? Give it to me now!*
>
> **Ich schenke meinem Onkel einen Hut. Ich gebe ihn ihm morgen.**
>
> *I'm giving my uncle a hat. I'm giving it to him tomorrow.*

ÜBUNG F	**Mach's jetzt!** You are losing your patience with your brother. You've asked him politely and he still isn't giving their things back to your friends. Now complete the same exercise as above, but be much more forceful. Use pronouns only.

EXAMPLE: sein Mantel / dein Freund Robert
Gib **ihn ihm!**

1. _____

2. _____

3. _____

4. _____

5. _____

NOTE: The direct and indirect objects do not have to be next to each other, as long as they are in the correct order relative to each other. You may place any element you wish to stress in the first position of a sentence, even the direct or indirect object. The second element is the verb and then the rules of word order apply.

> **Der Hut? Ihn gebe ich meinem Onkel.**   *The hat? I'm giving it to my uncle.*

7.   Dative Verbs

Certain verbs in German require a dative object rather than the customary accusative.

COMMON DATIVE VERBS					
antworten	to answer	**gehören**	to belong to	**passieren**	to happen
danken	to thank	**gehorchen**	to obey	**schaden**	to harm
fehlen	to be missing	**glauben**	to believe (s.o.)	**verzeihen**	to pardon, forgive
folgen	to follow	**gratulieren**	to congratulate	**Leid tun**	to be sorry
gefallen	to please, to be pleasing to	**wehtun**	to hurt (sep. prefix)	**zuhören**	to listen to (sep. prefix)

Folge mir! Du darfst mir helfen.	*Follow me. You may help me.*
Wir gratulieren dir.	*We congratulate you.*
Wer kann mir antworten?	*Who can answer me?*
Das Kind gehorcht seiner Mama.	*The child obeys his mother.*
Das Buch gehört meinem Sohn.	*The book belongs to my son.*

ÜBUNG G   **Die Engel.** It's later that evening and you are chatting on instant messenger to your friend. His sister and brother are angels. He's telling you about them.

EXAMPLE: mein Bruder / meine Eltern / immer / gehorchen
Mein Bruder gehorcht **meinen** Eltern immer.

1. meine Schwester / meine Mutter / immer / helfen

   _____

2. mein Bruder / meine Tennisfreunde / immer / gratulieren

   _____

3. meine Schwester / ich / immer / zuhören

   _____

4. mein Bruder / sein Freund / oft / helfen

   _____

5. die zwei / meine Freunde / sehr gut / gefallen

   _____

8.   Dative Idioms

Dative verbs are commonly used in expressing pleasure, sorrow, and discomfort:

a. Expressing likes and dislikes

There are several ways to express likes and dislikes. One of the most common is to use the verb *gefallen* – "to be pleasing."

Deine Bluse gefällt mir.   *I like your blouse.*
                                       (literally: Your blouse is pleasing to me.)

Gefällt dir mein Mantel?   *Do you like my coat?*

Nein, die Bluse gefällt ihr nicht. *No, she doesn't like the blouse.*

ÜBUNG H	**Deine Geburtstagsgeschenke.** Tell your mother what you think about the gifts you received for your birthday. Be honest. You don't have to like everything.

EXAMPLE: das rote Kleid   Das rote Kleid **gefällt** mir.   or
                              Das rote Kleid **gefällt** mir **nicht**.

          die Bonbons   Die Bonbons **gefallen** mir.   or
                              Die Bonbons **gefallen** mir **nicht**.

1. das Fahrrad

    _____

2. die Tennisschuhe

    _____

3. die Spielkarten

    _____

4. der Schokoladenkuchen

    _____

5. die Bluse

    _____

ÜBUNG I	**Wie gefallen deine Geschenke deinen Gästen?** The guests at your birthday party also expressed their opinion of your gifts. Your mother is interested in their reaction. Tell her what each person thought of them.

EXAMPLE: das Kleid / deine Tante   Das Kleid gefällt **meiner** Tante nicht.

1. das Fahrrad / mein Onkel /

    _____

2. die Tennisschuhe / meine Großeltern /

    _____

3. die Spielkarten / du /

    _____

4. der Schokoladenkuchen / meine Freundin Bärbel /

    _____

5. die Bluse / sie (they) /

    _____

b. Expressing sorrow or regret.

Es tut mir leid.	*I'm sorry.*
Es tut ihm leid.	*He's sorry.*
Tut's dir leid?	*Are you sorry?*

ÜBUNG J   **Sich entschuldigen.** Several people were sorry that they couldn't make your party. They called and left a message with your mother. What does she say to you? Use the people listed to the left as a list of those who called.

EXAMPLE: meine Geschichtslehrerin   Es tut **ihr** leid.

1. deine Deutschklubfreunde

_____

2. deine Oma

_____

3. die Mäder Zwillinge

_____

4. Herr Schmidt

_____

5. der Trainer

_____

ÜBUNG K   **Weitere Entschuldigungen.** More of your invited guests called after you got home and you spoke to them yourself. What exact words did each person use to tell you they were sorry that they would not be at the party?

EXAMPLE: deine Geschichtslehrerin   Es tut **mir** leid.

1. dein Cousin aus Berlin

_____

2. dein Onkel und deine Tante aus Genf

_____

3. deine Schwester in Bochum

_____

4. Herr Schmidt

_____

c. Expressing Comfort or Discomfort

Wie geht es Ihnen? Wie geht es dir/euch?	*How are you?*
Es geht mir gut.	*I'm fine.*

Es ist mir heiß / kalt / warm / kühl.	*I'm hot / cold / warm / cool.*
Es tut mir weh.	*It hurts (me).*
Mein Kopf tut mir weh.	*My head hurts. (singular)*
Meine Augen tun mir weh.	*My eyes hurt. (plural)*

ÜBUNG L **Beschwerden. (Complaints.)** You have a very vocal **Tante**. She complains about almost everything. Write answers to the questions showing her very negative outlook.

EXAMPLE: Wie geht es dir, Tante Emma?   **Mir** geht es sehr schlecht.

1. Wie ist dein Arm? _____

2. Wie geht es deinen Beinen? _____

3. Und deinen Augen? _____

4. Tut dir noch etwas weh? _____

5. Ist es dir im Zimmer bequem? _____

ÜBUNG M **Darf ich bitte zu Hause bleiben?** You haven't been feeling well, and might have stayed up a little late last night. Herr Frank is giving a quiz today. What can you say to your mother to convince her to let you stay home from school for the day? Give at least 5 reasons before she can interrupt you.

_____

_____

_____

_____

_____

CHAPTER 9
Prepositions

1. Prepositions

A preposition expresses a relationship between two things. In the sentences below, both *in* and *mit* are prepositions.

Meine Mutter ist in dem Park. Mein Bruder ging mit ihr.

My mother is in the park. My brother went with her.

2. Dative Prepositions

The following prepositions require a dative object.

PREPOSITIONS WHICH ALWAYS TAKE THE DATIVE CASE							
aus	*out, out of*	**ausser**	*except (for), with the exception of*	**bei**	*at the home of, near*	**mit**	*with*
nach	*after, to with geographic location*	**seit**	*since (temporal)*	**von**	*of, from*	**zu**	*to, toward*

Ausser meiner Mutter sind wir alle hier.   *We're all here except my mother.*

Sie rennen aus der Schule mit ihren Büchern.   *They are running out of the school with their books.*

ÜBUNG A   **Eine Bildergeschichte.** Your workgroup is writing a picture story but the picture cards all got separated from their sentences. Can you sort them out?

A

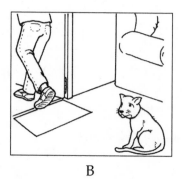

B

C

D

E

F

1. Wir essen heute Abend bei meinen Grosseltern. _____ F _____

2. Mein Opa kommt aus Schwaben und macht gute Suppen. _____

3. Ausser meiner Katze ist die ganze Familie dort. _____

4. Mein Cousin ist auch dort mit seiner Freundin. _____

5. Meine Oma kocht gut. Seit letzter Woche warte ich auf diesen Tag. _____

6. Der süsse Duft von Apfelkuchen grüsst uns an der Tür. _____

ÜBUNG B   **Ein Brief aus der Vergangenheit.** While you're there, your grandmother reads a letter from a former classmate who'd found her address on the Internet. She was reading it while cooking and it's gotten smudged. Can you help her decipher the letter? Use the word prompts to complete her letter.

aus – ausser – bei – bei – mit – nach – seit – von – zu

Ich wohne __mit__ meinem Mann, meinem Sohn und zwei Katzen. Wir wohnen _____ vielen

Jahren in Kiel. Mein Mann ist _____ Memmingen, einer Kleinstadt _____ Kiel. _____

meiner Tochter wohnt unsre ganze Familie noch _____ uns. Sie geht _____ der

Kunsthochschule in Bochum und hat eine Wohnung dort. She fährt oft am Wochenende

_____ Kiel und besucht uns. Sie bringt uns dann gute Sachen _____ dem Samstagsmarkt

am Rathaus. Und wie geht es dir?

ÜBUNG C   **Ein Worträtsel.** You go home and discover that your friend Heike has sent you a puzzle. All the endings are missing. You can fill in the blanks because you know the dative endings.

EXAMPLE: Markus wohnt bei d__en__ Feldhauers

1. Er trinkt Orangensaft aus ein_____ Glas.

2. Nach d_____ Orangensaft isst er eine Wurst mit ein_____ Gabel.

3. Er kriegt die Wurst von sein_____ Tante.

4. Sie kommt von d_____ Arbeit um vier Uhr.

5. Meine Tante geht oft zu_____ Arzt.

NOTE: If you wish to add variety to your writing, try using the contractions *zum (zu dem)* and *zur (zu der)* when working with dative prepositions.

| ÜBUNG D | **Das Fussballspiel.** Helga also asks you some questions about the upcoming soccer game. Answer them using at least one preposition from the list above in each sentence. If you need to review the dative endings, you'll find the charts on pages 55, 56, 57, 73.

EXAMPLE: Bekommst du eine Karte zum Fußballspiel? Eine Freundin gibt sie dir. / von
Ja, ich bekomme eine Karte **von einer** Freundin.

1. Wohin fahrt ihr zum Spiel?   Das Spiel ist in Altenholz. / nach

_____

2. Wie kommt ihr zum Spiel?   Der Bus fährt dorthin. / mit

_____

3. Kommen alle deine Freunde mit?   Ein Mädchen kommt nicht mit. / ausser

_____

4. Wie lange kennst du deinen Freund?   Du hast ihn im April kennengelernt / seit

_____

5. Wo esst ihr nach dem Spiel?   Ihr geht zu Schneiders. / zu

_____

3.   Accusative Prepositions

The following prepositions require an accusative object.

PREPOSITIONS WHICH ALWAYS TAKE THE ACCUSATIVE CASE					
*bis	*until, up to*	durch	*through*	für	*for*
gegen	*against, around or about (temporal)*	ohne	*without*	um	*at (temporal), around (locational)*

NOTE: You will often see *bis* combined with other prepositions. When that occurs, the article is in the case governed by the second preposition.

Ich laufe bis zur Bank. *I'll walk to the bank.*
Der Mann joggt durch den Park. *The man is jogging through the park.*
Wir kaufen es für unsere Mutter. *We'll buy it our mother.*
Ich bleibe bis April bei dir. *I'm staying until April at your house.*

ÜBUNG E | **Noch ein Rätsel.** Heike has sent you another puzzle. This time you need to fill in the correct accusative prepositions based on meaning. Use the words from the word bank to choose your answers.

bis – durch – für – gegen – ohne – ~~um~~ – um

EXAMPLE: Er geht __um__ sechs Uhr.

1. Sascha geht heute _____ den Park.

2. Er geht _____ seinen Regenmantel.

3. _____ vier Uhr beginnt es zu regnen.

4. Er kann nichts _____ den Regen machen.

5. _____ Sascha ist das nicht gut.

6. Sein Hemd bleibt _____ Abend noch nass.

ÜBUNG F | **Deine Geschichte.** You decide to show Heike that you do understand your prepositions. You take her word list (from *Übung E*) and create a story using each one at least once. There are many topics possible: an event upcoming at school, your day, things you can do in your town, etc. Email her your short story with all the endings correct.

_____

_____

_____

_____

_____

ÜBUNG G | **Heike gibt nicht auf.** (Heike won't give up.) Heike still wants to send you puzzles. This time she wrote a story using both accusative and dative prepositions. And once again she wants you to fill in the correct endings.

EXAMPLE: Mercedes geht zu __der__ Schule.
Sie geht nur um __die__ Ecke.

1. Mercedes fährt mit d_____ Bus.

2. Außer d_____ Busfahrerin ist sie allein.

3. Der Bus fährt durch ein_____ Wald.

4. Nach d_____ Wald kommt eine Wiese.

5. Von d_____ Bus kann Mercedes viel sehen.

6. Durch d_____ Fenster sieht sie etwas Interessantes.

7. Aber ohne ihr_____ Brille kann sie es nicht gut sehen.

8. Die Busfahrt ist eine besonders schöne Fahrt für ein_____ Sonntagnachmittag.

4.   Two-way Prepositions

The following prepositions require a dative object if they express location and answer the question "where" (*wo*). They take accusative if they express motion towards a goal and answer the question "where to" (*wohin*).

Mein Cousin springt in das Wasser.	**Meine Tante geht in die Bäckerei.**	**Mein Onkel läuft in den Park.**
My cousin is jumping into the water.	*My aunt is going into the bakery.*	*My uncle runs into the park.*
Jetzt steht er in dem Wasser.	**Jetzt ist sie in der Bäckerei.**	**Jetzt übt er in dem Park.**
Now he is standing in the water.	*Now she is in the bakery.*	*Then he exercises in the park.*

PREPOSITIONS WHICH TAKE EITHER THE DATIVE OR ACCUSATIVE					
an	out	**auf**	except (for), with the exception of	**hinter**	behind
in	in, into	**neben**	next to, near	**über**	over, about, above, across
unter	under, among	**vor**	before, in front of	**zwischen**	of, from

5.   Expressing Location

The two-way prepositions, when used with the dative case, describe where something or someone is.

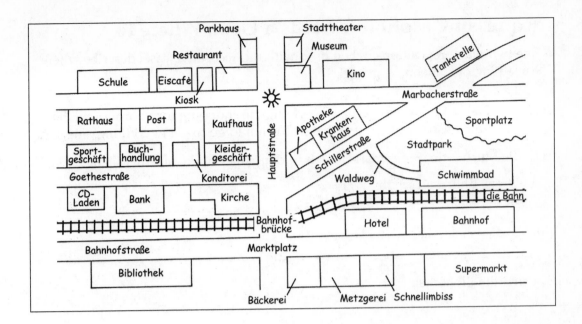

ÜBUNG H   **Wo ist . . .?** You are hosting an exchange student who wishes to go into town. She has given you a list of places she wants to visit. Describe where each is using the above map. There will be several different ways to describe the location of each store.

EXAMPLE: das Eiscafé   Es ist **neben der Schule.**

1. das Museum _____

2. das Kleidergeschäft _____

3. die Bibliothek _____

4. die Post_____

5. die Buchhandlung _____

ÜBUNG I   **Das verlorene Mathebuch.** Your brother has lost his math book in your house. Suggest at least five places that it might be.

EXAMPLE: Ist es **hinter der Couch?**
          Ist es **in der Küche?**

1. _____

2. _____

3. _____

4. _____

5. _____

6.   Expressing Motion towards a Goal, Where to

The two-way prepositions, when used with the accusative case, describe where something or someone is going.

ÜBUNG J | **Deine Einkaufsliste.** You are doing the shopping for your mother. She gives you a list and suggests where you should go to get everything. She says:

EXAMPLE: die Milch / der Supermarkt   Geh **in den** Supermarkt **für die** Milch!

1. Blumen / das Blumengeschäft

_____

2. die neue CD von Sascha / der CD-Laden

_____

3. ein Buch / die Bibliothek

_____

4. eine Medizin / die Apotheke

_____

5. den neuen Fahrplan / der Bahnhof

_____

ÜBUNG K | **Ein Tag in der Stadt.** You have decided to go with your friend to the city for the day. Suggest an itinerary, visiting at least 5 stores or institutions before coming home.

EXAMPLE: Wir gehen zuerst in das Museum. Dann gehen wir in das Restaurant.

1. _____
2. _____
3. _____
4. _____
5. _____

ÜBUNG L | **Ein Spiel.** In order to practice the two-way prepositions you create a game for yourself. You write sentence pairs that are similar, but one contains a verb of motion towards a goal. The other verb describes a location. Write at least six sentence pairs.

EXAMPLE: der Stuhl /hinter   Sie **geht hinter den** Stuhl.
                              Sie **steht hinter dem** Stuhl.

          Die Kirche / vor   Er **läuft vor die** Kirche.
                              Er **ist vor der** Kirche.

1. das Haus/neben   _____

   _____

2. der Garten/in   _____

   _____

3. das Dach/auf   _____

   _____

4. *Your choices*   _____

   _____

5.   _____

   _____

6.   _____

   _____

ÜBUNG M **Die letzte Email von Heike.** Heike has sent you her final preposition exercise. She has written a story with many prepositions from all three types. Your challenge is to fill in the correct dative or accusative endings and then to write an ending for the story using more prepositions.

EXAMPLE: Ute und Uwe gehen durch d__en__ Wald.

Ute und Uwe gehen um ein_____ Ecke. Sie sehen einen Wolf. Er sitzt auf ein_____ Stuhl.

Auf d_____ Stuhl liegt auch eine Decke. Uwe und Ute wollen nicht mit d_____ Wolf

sprechen, aber der Wolf sagt zu ihn_____ , „Warum sind Sie in mein_____ Wald?" Ute sagt

zu d_____ Wolf, „Wir wollen nur spazieren gehen." Der Wolf hat Hunger. In sein_____

Tasche hat er ein Wurstbrot. Er will das Brot mit d_____ Kinder_____ teilen. Er fragt,

„Hat außer m_____ jemand Hunger?"

_____

_____

_____

_____

_____

CHAPTER 10
Adjective Endings

1. Adjectives following a linking verb (*Ich bin intelligent und nett.*) are easy to use in German. They take no endings.

2. Some common adjectives to use when describing a person are: *aktiv, intelligent, neugierig, nett, freundlich, hilfsbereit, toll, sportlich, gesund, krank, energisch, lang, kurz, schlank, dick, blonde, brunette, blauäugig, dunkel, hell, schnell, langsam, gross, klein, jung, alt, altmodisch, und schick.*

| ÜBUNG A | **Du über dich.** You're planning a trip to Austria as an exchange student. Write an email to your host family describing yourself and your personality. Discuss at least ten attributes that make you unique. |

_____

_____

_____

_____

_____

_____

_____

| ÜBUNG B | **Die Familie über die Familie.** Within a week you had an answer to your email. The mother wrote and described her entire family: two parents, three children and a grandmother. What did her answer to you say? Write at least one sentence about each member of the family. |

_____

_____

_____

_____

_____

_____

_____

1. Adjectives Which Precede a Noun

Adjectives do not always follow a linking verb. Often they appear before the noun they modify. In that case, you must add endings to the adjective depending upon the noun that it modifies.

Mein kleiner Bruder is drei Jahre alt. *My little brother is three years old.*
Der dunkelblaue Rock passt gut. *The dark blue skirt fits well.*
Die weiße Bluse ist zu klein. *The white blouse is too small.*

2. Adjectives Preceded by a Definite Article

Adjectives sandwiched between the definite article (*der/die/das*) and a noun end either in *–e* or *–en*.

Der alte Mann trägt den grauen Anzug.
The old man is wearing the gray suit.

Die junge Frau hat die blaugepunktete Bluse an.
The young woman has the blue polka-dotted blouse on.

Das kleine Kind trägt das rotkarierte Hemd.
The small child is wearing the red checkered shirt.

	MASCULINE	FEMININE	NEUTER	PLURAL
Nom	der rot-e	die rot-e	das rot-e	die rot-en
Dat	dem rot-en	der rot-en	dem rot-en	den rot-en
Akk	den rot-en	die rot-e	das rot-e	die rot-en

ÜBUNG C **Die Eine Modenschau.** (A fashion show.) You took your younger sister and her friends shopping. They are discussing the latest fashions. You ask her what she thinks about the clothes they are seeing. They answer:

EXAMPLE: Wie findest du den roten Mantel dort?   **Der rote** Mantel ist toll!

1. Wie findest du die blaue Jacke in der Ecke? (zu langweilig)

   _____

2. Und die braunen Schuhe dort? (Klasse)

   _____

3. Und wie findest du die blaugepunktete Bluse? (prima)

   _____

4. Das rote Hemd. Wie findest du es? (nur so lala)

   _____

5. Und der rosa Anorak? Magst du ihn? (fantastisch)

   _____

| ÜBUNG D | **Schaufensterbummeln.** Later on in the week you and your cousin are looking at a display window in a clothing boutique. You're discussing the outfits you see with her. There are several outfits. In order to avoid confusion, mention each outfit by its color. Give your opinion of the articles of clothing mentioned. |

EXAMPLE: Pulli / blau / dir gefallen   **Der blaue** Pulli gefällt mir.
Jacke / rot / spitze / finden.   Ich finde **die rote** Jacke Spitze.

1. Bluse / weiß / nicht schön / finden.

_____

2. Hose / grün / nicht / mögen

_____

3. Mantel / rot / schick / sein

_____

4. Gürtel / schwarz / zu dick / finden

_____

5. Jacke / gelb / dir gefallen

_____

6. Pulli / schwarz / auch / mögen

_____

| ÜBUNG E | **Die Frau mit der . . . .** You turn to look at what people around you are wearing. So that your cousin knows where to look, refer to each of them by something they are wearing. |

EXAMPLE: Frau / blau / Bluse   die Frau **mit der blauen Bluse**

1. Mann / schwarz / Hut

_____

2. Kind / blaugestreift / Hemdchen

_____

3. Mädchen / schick / Mantel

_____

4. Zwillinge / gelb / Gummistiefel

_____

5. der alte Mann / laut / Krawatte

_____

3. Adjectives Preceded by an Indefinite Article

Adjectives sandwiched between the indefinite article (*ein/eine/ein*) or a possessive adjective (*mein, dein,* etc.) and a noun end in either *-er, -es, -e* or *-en*.

	MASCULINE	FEMININE	NEUTER	PLURAL
Nom	ein rot-er	eine rot-e	ein rot-es	meine rot-en
Dat	einem rot-en	einer rot-en	einem rot-en	meinen rot-en
Akk	einen rot-en	eine rot-e	ein rot-es	meine rot-en

ÜBUNG F | **Die Farben.** Your pen pal Dirk has asked you to add colors to his list of clothing items he wants to buy.

EXAMPLE: eine Hose/schwarz   eine schwarze Hose

1. ein Hemd / rot _____

2. ein Pulli / grün _____

3. eine Krawatte / blau _____

4. ein Gürtel / braun _____

5. eine Unterhose / weiß _____

6. eine Jacke / schwarz _____

7. ein T-Shirt / rot _____

ÜBUNG G | **Dirk geht Einkaufen.** Dirk went shopping. He then emails you a picture showing you his new clothes (and his new girlfriend). You're talking on the phone to a friend, describe their outfits. Use adjectives such as *gestreift, gepunktet, kariert, schick, altmodisch, langweilig, toll, Klasse, Spitze,* and of course, even though he sent you the picture in black and white, you could add colors to your descriptions. You should create at least five sentences for each of them, so that your friend can create a picture for himself.

EXAMPLE: **Sie trägt eine weisse Bluse mit einem gestreiften Kragen.**

1. Sie _____

_____

_____

_____

_____

2. Er _____

_____

_____

_____

_____

| ÜBUNG H | **Schick oder schlampig?** (Chic or sloppy?) If you are working on this book with a partner, here's where you can have some fun. Imagine a fully-clothed person. It may be a man, woman, boy or girl, real or imaginary. Write a complete description of that person. Then read that description to your partner and have him or her draw the person you have imagined. How close did he or she get to the person you actually described? |

_____

_____

_____

_____

_____

_____

_____

_____

CHAPTER 11

Compound Sentences
Expressing Knowledge

In German, it is easy to combine two thoughts into one sentence. These are then called compound sentences.

1. Compound Sentences with Independent (Main) Clauses

a. Compound sentences can be created using *und* (and) and *aber* (but) to introduce the second clause. Each of the two independent clauses can stand alone as a sentence.

Wir essen im Restaurant und dann gehen wir ins Kino.

We are eating in the restaurant and then we are going to the movies.

Die Feier beginnt um 8 Uhr, aber ich kann erst um 9 Uhr kommen.

The party begins at 8 o'clock, but I can't come until 9 o'clock.

b. When combining independent clauses using *und* and *aber*, each maintains normal word order. The verb remains the second element in its clause.

NOTE: There is no comma before the conjunction when using *und*.
There is a comma before the conjunction when using *aber*.

ÜBUNG A | **Meine Klassenkameraden.** You are writing a letter to your pen pal about your classmates. Now that your German skills are better you do not want to write only simple sentences. Combine the following sentences using *und*.

EXAMPLE: Simone spielt Tennis. Sie ist auch eine gute Fußballerin.
Simone spielt Tennis **und** sie ist auch eine gute Fußballerin.

1. Bastian spielt Basketball. Er ist auch Fußballer.

   _____

2. Jennifer ist Schachmeisterin. Sie spielt Handball.

   _____

3. David spielt Klavier. Er ist nicht sehr sportlich.

   _____

4. Martin ist sehr nett. Er ist der Klassensprecher.

   _____

5. Jakob liest sehr viel. Er kann auch gut schreiben.

   _____

| ÜBUNG B | **Meine Klassenkamaderen, aber.** You continue your letter but now you are writing about apparent contradictions in you friends. You must use *aber* to connect the sentences. |

EXAMPLE: Simone spielt keinen Sport. Sie ist sportlich.
Simone spielt keinen Sport, **aber** sie ist sportlich.

1. Gregor ist sehr nett. Er spricht zu viel.

_____

2. Silvia ist sehr intelligent. Sie kriegt immer schlechte Noten.

_____

3. Lars spielt immer Fußball. Er ist nicht sehr gut.

_____

4. Tanja will Lehrerin werden. Sie hat die Schule nicht gern.

_____

5. Heike geht auf die Uni. Sie arbeitet im Museum.

_____

2.   Compound Sentences with a Dependent Clause

In some compound sentences only one clause can stand alone as a complete sentence. The second clause, called the dependent clause, is introduced by *dass* (that) or *weil* (because) and is not a complete sentence on its own.

Meine Freundin sagt, dass sie nicht kommt.

My friend says that she isn't coming.

Wir fahren nicht, weil mein Rad kaputt ist.

We aren't riding because my bicycle is broken.

When combining two clauses using *dass* or *weil*, the independent clause maintains normal word order. The verb in the dependent clause goes to the end of its clause.

NOTE: There is a comma before both *dass* and *weil*.

Ich komme nicht. + Ich bin krank. = Ich komme nicht, weil ich krank bin.

I am not coming. + I am sick. = I am not coming because I am sick.

Ihr wisst. + Wir spielen am Montag Fussball. = Ihr wisst, dass wir am Montag Fussball spielen.

You know. + We are playing soccer on Monday. = You know, that we are playing soccer on Monday.

ÜBUNG C   **Der Hund hat meine Hausaufgaben gegessen.** (The dog ate my homework.) It is Monday and many of your classmates and even the teacher forgot to bring things to school. Join the columns with *weil* to write the excuses they are giving.

EXAMPLE: Herr Petzhold hat keinen Kuli, **weil sein Kuli kaputt ist.**

Maya hat keinen Bleistift.   Sie bringt immer das falsche Buch.

Julie hat ihr Mathebuch nicht.   Es ist noch in der Wäsche.

Martin hat die Schultasche nicht.   **weil**   Er hat heute Morgen Eile.

Jens hat sein Turnzeug heute nicht.   Sein Kuli ist kaputt.

Herr Petzhold hat keinen Kuli.   Sie vergisst ihn immer.

1. _____

2. _____

3. _____

4. _____

5. _____

ÜBUNG D   **Ein Bild ist 1000 Wörter wert.** (A picture's worth a thousand words.) Your classmates are giving excuses for not being able to go on a class trip. They have sent you pictures explaining their problems. Use the pictures to write out their excuses.

EXAMPLE: Martin kann nicht mitkommen.
             Martin kann nicht kommen, **weil er Kopfschmerzen hat.**

1. Ursula kann nicht mitkommen.

_____

2. Connie kann auch nicht mitfahren.

_____

3. Karl darf nicht mitkommen.

_____

4. Jens will nicht mitkommen.

_____

5. Marlies will auch nicht mitkommen.

_____

ÜBUNG E | **Ja, wir wissen, was wir tun müssen.** You are planning a school trip. You must write a report for your teacher in which you assure him that everyone knows what to do. Use the sentence elements to create your list.

EXAMPLE: Thomas / wissen + die Karten / kaufen
Thomas weiss, **dass** er die Karten **kauft**.

1. Gabi / wissen + das Essen / besorgen

_____

2. Gerd / wissen + die Getränke / bringen

_____

3. Friedrich und Eva / wissen + die Fahrkarten / kaufen

_____

4. Herr Biedermeier / wissen + alle Eltern / anrufen

_____

5. Leon / wissen + die Liste / schreiben

_____

3.   Compound Sentences with Modal Verbs

Very often the compound sentences are used with modal verbs.

The rules of word order do not change. In the main clause, the verb is the second element and the infinitive completer goes to the end of its clause. In the dependent clause, the verb goes to the end.

Er kann nicht kommen, weil er kein Geld hat.

He cannot come because he has no money.

ÜBUNG F | **Ein Bericht für den Lehrer.** (A report for the teacher.) Now you are reading the excuses that some students have written. You must put the sentences together before giving them to your teacher.

EXAMPLE: (Georg schreibt) Ich kann nicht mitkommen. Ich bekomme Besuch.
Georg kann nicht mitkommen, **weil er** Besuch **bekommt.**

1. (Tilden) Ich kann nicht mitkommen. Ich habe kein Geld.

   _____

2. (Marlies) Ich will nicht mitkommen. Ich habe keine Lust dazu.

   _____

3. (Gerd und Gerda) Wir dürfen nicht mitkommen. Die Mutti ist krank.

   _____

4. (Laura) Ich kann nicht mitkommen. Ich spiele Tennis am Dienstag.

   _____

5. (Leonie) Ich darf nicht mitfahren. Ich habe einen Termin beim Arzt.

   _____

NOTE: If the modal is in the dependent clause, the modal goes to the end of the clause after the infinitive completer.

> **Wissen Sie, dass ich morgen nicht arbeiten kann?**
>
> *Do you know that I cannot work tomorrow?*

ÜBUNG G | **Die Gedanken sind frei.** (Thoughts are free.) Use *weil* to join the two sentences and tell what each person is thinking.

EXAMPLE: Ich komme nicht mit. Georg kann nicht mitkommen.
Ich komme nicht mit, **weil Georg nicht mitkommen kann.**

1. Ich will nicht mitkommen. Marlies will nicht mitkommen.

   _____

2. Ich darf nicht mitfahren. Tilden kann nicht mitkommen.

   _____

3. Herr Marzipan ist nicht froh. Gerd und Gerda dürfen nicht mitkommen.

   _____

4. Tilden will nicht gehen. Laura kann nicht gehen.

   _____

5. Lena kommt nicht mit. Sie muss Tennis spielen.

   _____

ÜBUNG H | **Weißt du was?** You must check with a number of different people to make sure that they understand why some people are not coming along. Form questions with *wissen* based on the information.

EXAMPLE: (Peter) Georg kann nicht mitkommen
          Peter, weisst du, dass Georg nicht mitkommen **kann**?

1. (Peter und Marlies) Gerd und Gerda dürfen nicht mitkommen.

   _____

2. (Herr Marzipan) Marlies will nicht mitkommen.

   _____

3. (Laura) Tilden kann nicht mitkommen.

   _____

4. (Tilden) Laura kann nicht mitkommen.

   _____

5. (Sophie) Paul darf nicht mitkommen.

   _____

ÜBUNG I	**Eine Liste.** Your classmates are giving Herr Marzipan many excuses. Make a list of the top five excuses for not being able to attend Herr Marzipan's make-up class on Friday afternoon.

EXAMPLE: Ich kann nicht kommen, **weil ich arbeiten muss.**
          Meine Mutti sagt, **dass ich mein Zimmer aufräumen muss.**

1. _____
2. _____
3. _____
4. _____
5. _____

4.   Expressing Knowledge

English has only one word for "to know." We say: "I know you" or "I know that two plus two is four." In German, each of these different meanings of "know" is a different word.

a. *kennen* = to be acquainted with someone or something.

Ich kenne Hamburg gut.	*I know Hamburg well.*
Ja, ich kenne Josef Behringer.	*Yes, I know Joseph Behringer.*

b. *wissen* = to know a fact, often combined with an independent clause.

Weißt du, wann der Film zu Ende ist?

Do you know when the movie is over?

NOTE: The verb *wissen* is irregular. See chart below.

SINGULAR	PLURAL
ich weiß	wir wiss - en
du weiß - t	ihr wiss – t
er, sie, es weiss	sie wiss - en
Sie wiss - en	

ÜBUNG J	**Wissen ist Macht.** (Knowledge is Power.) Your friend wrote you a note that got wet and smudged in the rain. Try to fill in the missing words with *kennen* or *wissen*.

Heute Abend läuft ein neuer Film. ___**Kennst**___ du den Film? Ich _____ nicht wann

er beginnt. Die Schauspielerin in dem Film heißt Mala Davidsin. _____ du sie? Ich

nicht. Ich _____ auch den Schauspieler Hans Hansenberger nicht. _____ du,

wo das Kino ist? Es ist in der Kinogasse. Ich _____ , dass du mitkommen willst.

Sollen wir um 7.00 Uhr gehen? Bis dahin,

Dein

Fritz

ÜBUNG K	**Ein Fragenspiel.** You are preparing for a question game in your German class. Your goal is to write 6 question pairs. One question concerning whether your classmate "knows about" or is "acquainted with" someone or some thing and a question of fact about this person or thing. Your sentence pairs might look like these: Do you know Arnold Schwarzenegger? *Kennst du Arnold Schwarzenegger?* Do you know how old he is? *Weisst du, wie alt er ist?*

EXAMPLE: **Kennst du New York City?   Weisst du, wie groß es ist?**
Kennst du Mariah Carey?   Weisst du, was sie singt?

1. _____

2. _____

3. _____

4. _____

5. _____

6. _____

CHAPTER 12

The Past Tense of *Sein*
The Past Tense of *Haben*

Until now you have only been able to express present or future actions. Adding *was/were* and *had* to your vocabulary inventory allows you to talk about events which occurred in the past. The past tense of both verbs is irregular and will have to be memorized.

1. The Past Tense of *Sein*

Sein is the infinitive of the verb "to be". The present tense translates as "am," "is" or "are." The past tense translates as "was" or "were."

SINGULAR		PLURAL	
ich war	*I was*	**wir war –en**	*we were*
du war – st	*you (informal) were*	**ihr war–t**	*you (informal) were*
er, sie, es war	*he, she, or it was*	**sie war –en**	*they were*
	Sie war – en	*You (formal) were*	

ÜBUNG A | **Ein Tag in der Stadt.** While visiting in Basel, Switzerland, you went downtown with your friends. Write a postcard home telling your parents what you did. Use the words *zuerst* (first), *dann* (then) and *zuletzt* (last, at last) in your narrative.

EXAMPLE: Bäckerei/Buchladen . . .

> **Zuerst waren** wir in der Bäckerei.
> Dann waren wir **in dem Buchladen.**

Post – Supermarkt – Kirche – Stadtpark – Sporthalle

_____

_____

_____

_____

_____

ÜBUNG B **Wo warst du an dem Abend?** You are having a mock trial in class and your assignment is to take a survey of where everyone was last night. Ask some people directly and about others. Write the correct question for the person(s) on the list.

EXAMPLE: Herr Schmidt? **Wo waren Sie** an dem Abend, Herr Schmidt.
Michaela? (about Jens) **Wo war er** an dem Abend?

1. Jonas? _____

2. Lucas und Lena? _____

3. Anna? (about David) _____

4. David? (about Marie) _____

5. Jakob? (about Marie and David) _____

2. The Past Tense of *haben*

Haben is the infinitive form of the verb "to have." Its past tense translates as "had."

SINGULAR		PLURAL	
ich hatte	*I had*	**wir hatt –en**	*we had*
du hatt – est	*you (informal) had*	**ihr hatt – et**	*you (informal) had*
er, sie, es hatt – e	*he, she, or it had*	**sie hatt –en**	*they had*
	Sie hatt – en	*You (formal) had*	

ÜBUNG C **Probleme?** You had problems last night with your assignment for the Schulfest. You asked others who were assigned duties what their experience had been. Form the correct questions.

EXAMPLE: Gerd / du   Gerd, **hattest du** gestern Probleme?

1. Herr Schmidt / Sie _____

2. Fritz und Franceska / ihr _____

3. Olli / du _____

4. Frau Ratzlaf / Sie _____

| ÜBUNG D | **Entschuldigungen.** Many of your classmates did not attend the *Schulfest* last night. Now your teacher has asked you to find out why not. Put the words in the columns together to determine why each person stayed away. |

EXAMPLE: **Marco hatte keine Zeit.**

Marco	kein Geld
Kamille	keine Zeit
Veronika	keine Lust
Harald	viele Hausaufgaben
Samuel	Tennistraining
Gerd und Gerda	Klavierunterricht

1. _____

2. _____

3. _____

4. _____

5. _____

| ÜBUNG E | **Weitere Entschuldigungen.** Your classmates had so many excuses, that you decided to write some of them down for the Schulfestkommittee. Put the reasons in sentences using the past tense forms of *haben*. |

EXAMPLE: Herr Petzhold / keine Zeit   Herr Petzhold **hatte** keine Zeit.

1. Marianne / Kopfweh   _____

2. Felix / kein Geld   _____

3. Aimee und Maria / Termine   _____

4. Frau Fritz / Besuch   _____

5. du / Hausaufgaben in Deutsch _____

| ÜBUNG F | **Eine Email.** You and two of your friends went on an excursion to town. Write an email and tell your pen pal Erika what you did, where you were, and what the three of you each had for lunch. |

Hallo, Erika! _____

_____

_____

_____

_____

                                                   Dein Benjamin

Appendix – Grammar Reference Tables

1. Weak Verbs - Conjugation

hören- *to hear*

PRESENT TENSE	ich	höre
	du	hörst
	er, sie, es	hört
	wir	hören
	ihr	hört
	sie, Sie	hören
PAST TENSE	ich	hörte
	du	hörtest
	er, sie, es	hörte
	wir	hörten
	ihr	hörtet
	sie, Sie	hörten
FUTURE TENSE	ich	**werde** hören
	du	**wirst** hören
	er, sie, es	**wird** hören
	wir	**werden** hören
	ihr	**werdet** hören
	sie, Sie	**werden** hören
PRESENT PERFECT TENSE	ich	**habe** gehört
	du	**hast** gehört
	er, sie, es	**hat** gehört
	wir	**haben** gehört
	ihr	**habt** gehört
	sie, Sie	**haben** gehört

PAST PERFECT TENSE	ich	**hatte** gehört
	du	**hattest** gehört
	er, sie, es	**hatte** gehört
	wir	**hatten** gehört
	ihr	**hattet** gehört
	sie, Sie	**hatten** gehört
FUTURE PERFECT TENSE	ich	**werde** gehört **haben**
	du	**wirst** gehört **haben**
	er, sie, es	**wird** gehört **haben**
	wir	**werden** gehört **haben**
	ihr	**werdet** gehört **haben**
	sie, Sie	**werden** gehört **haben**
IMPERATIVE	du	Hör(e)!
	wir	Hören wir!
	ihr	Hört!
	sie, Sie	Hören Sie!

2.   Strong Verbs (Helping Verb = *haben*)

tragen, trägt, trug, hat getragen - to wear or carry

PRESENT TENSE	ich	trage
	du	trägst
	er, sie, es	trägt
	wir	tragen
	ihr	tragt
	sie, Sie	tragen
PAST TENSE	ich	trug
	du	trugst
	er, sie, es	trug
	wir	trugen
	ihr	trugt
	sie, Sie	trugen

FUTURE TENSE	ich	**werde** tragen
	du	**wirst** tragen
	er, sie, es	**wird** tragen
	wir	**werden** tragen
	ihr	**werdet** tragen
	sie, Sie	**werden** tragen
PRESENT PERFECT TENSE	ich	**habe** getragen
	du	**hast** getragen
	er, sie, es	**hat** getragen
	wir	**haben** getragen
	ihr	**habt** getragen
	sie, Sie	**haben** getragen
PAST PERFECT TENSE	ich	**hatte** getragen
	du	**hattest** getragen
	er, sie, es	**hatte** getragen
	wir	**hatten** getragen
	ihr	**hattet** getragen
	sie, Sie	**hatten** getragen
FUTURE PERFECT TENSE	ich	**werde** getragen **haben**
	du	**wirst** getragen **haben**
	er, sie, es	**wird** getragen **haben**
	wir	**werden** getragen **haben**
	ihr	**werdet** getragen **haben**
	sie, Sie	**werden** getragen **haben**
IMPERATIVE	du	Trag(e)!
	wir	Tragen wir!
	ihr	Tragt!
	sie, Sie	Tragen Sie!

3. Strong Verbs (Helping Verb = *sein*)

gehen, geht, ging, ist gegangen – to go

PRESENT TENSE	ich	geh**e**
	du	geh**st**
	er, sie, es	geh**t**
	wir	geh**en**
	ihr	geh**t**
	sie, Sie	geh**en**
PAST TENSE	ich	ging
	du	ging**st**
	er, sie, es	ging
	wir	ging**en**
	ihr	ging**t**
	sie, Sie	ging**en**
FUTURE TENSE	ich	**werde** gehen
	du	**wirst** gehen
	er, sie, es	**wird** gehen
	wir	**werden** gehen
	ihr	**werdet** gehen
	sie, Sie	**werden** gehen
PRESENT PERFECT TENSE	ich	**bin** gegangen
	du	**bist** gegangen
	er, sie, es	**ist** gegangen
	wir	**sind** gegangen
	ihr	**seid** gegangen
	sie, Sie	**sind** gegangen
PAST PERFECT TENSE	ich	**war** gegangen
	du	**warst** gegangen
	er, sie, es	**war** gegangen
	wir	**waren** gegangen
	ihr	**wart** gegangen
	sie, Sie	**waren** gegangen

FUTURE PERFECT TENSE	ich	**werde** gegangen **sein**
	du	**wirst** gegangen **sein**
	er, sie, es	**wird** gegangen **sein**
	wir	**werden** gegangen **sein**
	ihr	**werdet** gegangen **sein**
	sie, Sie	**werden** gegangen **sein**
IMPERATIVE	du	Geh(e)!
	wir	Gehen wir!
	ihr	Geht!
	sie, Sie	Gehen Sie!

4.   Strong Verbs – List of Principal Parts

PRINCIPAL PARTS OF STRONG VERBS

INFINITIVE	PRESENT TENSE THIRD PERSON SINGULAR	PAST TENSE FIRST AND THIRD PERSONS SINGULAR	PAST PARTICIPLE WITH HELPING VERB	ENGLISH MEANING
backen	bäckt	backte (buk)	hat gebacken	bake
befehlen	befiehlt	befahl	hat befohlen	command
beginnen	beginnt	begann	hat begonnen	begin
beißen	beißt	biss	hat gebissen	bite
bergen	birgt	barg	hat geborgen	hide, protect
betrügen	betrügt	betrog	hat betrogen	betray, deceive
biegen	biegt	bog	hat/ist gebogen	bend, turn
bieten	bietet	bot	hat geboten	offer
binden	bindet	band	hat gebunden	tie, bind
bitten	bittet	bat	hat gebeten	request, plea
blasen	blast	blies	hat geblasen	blow
bleiben	bleibt	blieb	ist geblieben	stay, remain
braten	brät	briet	hat gebraten	roast, fry
brechen	bricht	brach	hat gebrochen	break
brennen	brennt	brannte	hat gebrannt	burn
bringen	bringt	brachte	hat gebracht	bring

INFINITIVE	PRESENT TENSE THIRD PERSON SINGULAR	PAST TENSE FIRST AND THIRD PERSONS SINGULAR	PAST PARTICIPLE WITH HELPING VERB	ENGLISH MEANING
denken	denkt	dachte	hat gedacht	think
dringen	dringt	drang	hat/ist gedrungen	press forward
dürfen	darf	durfte	hat gedurft	may, be allowed to
empfehlen	empfiehlt	empfahl	hat empfohlen	recommend
erschrecken	erschrickt	erschrak	ist erschrocken	be startled
essen	isst	aß	hat gegessen	eat
fahren	fährt	fuhr	hat/ist gefahren	ride, drive
fallen	fällt	fiel	ist gefallen	fall
fangen	fängt	fing	hat gefangen	catch
findet	findet	fand	hat gefunden	find
fliegen	fliegt	flog	hat/ist geflogen	fly
fliehen	flieht	floh	ist geflohen	flee
fließen	fließt	floss	ist geflossen	flow
fressen	frisst	fraß	hat gefressen	eat (animal), devour
frieren	friert	fror	hat/ist gefroren	freeze
gebären	gebärt	gebar	hat geboren	give birth to
geben	gibt	gab	hat gegeben	give
gedeihen	gedeiht	gedieh	ist gediehen	grow, thrive
gehen	geht	ging	ist gegangen	go, walk
gelingen	gelingt	gelang	ist gelungen	succeed
gelten	gilt	galt	hat gegolten	be valid
genießen	genießt	genoss	hat genossen	enjoy
geschehen	geschieht	geschah	ist geschehen	happen
gewinnen	gewinnt	gewann	hat gewonnen	win
gießen	gießt	goss	hat gegossen	pour
gleichen	gleicht	glich	hat geglichen	resemble
gleiten	gleitet	glitt	ist geglitten	glide, slide
graben	gräbt	grub	hat gegraben	dig
greifen	greift	griff	hat gegriffen	grasp, grab
haben	hat	hatte	hat gehabt	have
halten	hält	hielt	hat gehalten	hold, stop
hängen	hängt	hing	hat gehangen	hang

INFINITIVE	PRESENT TENSE THIRD PERSON SINGULAR	PAST TENSE FIRST AND THIRD PERSONS SINGULAR	PAST PARTICIPLE WITH HELPING VERB	ENGLISH MEANING
hauen	haut	haute	hat gehauen	cut
heben	hebt	hob	hat gehoben	life, raise up
heissen	heisst	hiess	hat geheissen	be called
helfen	hilft	half	hat geholfen	help
kennen	kennt	kannte	hat gekonnt	know, be acquainted with
klingen	klingt	klang	hat geklungen	sound
kneifen	kneift	kniff	hat gekniffen	pinch
kommen	kommt	kam	ist gekommen	come
können	kann	konnte	hat gekonnt	can, be able to
kriechen	kriecht	kroch	ist gekrochen	crawl
laden	lädt	lud	hat geladen	load
lassen	lässt	liess	hat gelassen	let, leave, allow
laufen	läuft	lief	ist gelaufen	run, walk
leiden	leidet	litt	hat gelitten	suffer
lesen	liest	las	hat gelesen	read
liegen	liegt	lag	hat gelegen	lie
mahlen	mahlt	mahlte	hat gemahlen	grind
meiden	meidet	mied	hat gemieden	avoid
messen	misst	mass	hat gemessen	measure
misslingen	misslingt	misslang	ist misslungen	fail
mögen	mag	mochte	hat gemocht	like, like to
müssen	muss	musste	hat gemusst	must, have to
nehmen	nimmt	nahm	hat genommen	take
nennen	nennt	nannte	hat genannt	name
pfeifen	pfeift	pfiff	hat gepfiffen	whistle
preisen	preist	pries	hat gepriesen	praise
raten	rät	riet	hat geraten	advise, guess
reiben	reibt	rieb	hat gerieben	rub
reissen	reisst	riss	hat/ist gerissen	rip, tear
reiten	reitet	ritt	hat/ist geritten	ride (an animal)
rennen	rennt	rannte	ist gerannt	run

INFINITIVE	PRESENT TENSE THIRD PERSON SINGULAR	PAST TENSE FIRST AND THIRD PERSONS SINGULAR	PAST PARTICIPLE WITH HELPING VERB	ENGLISH MEANING
riechen	riecht	roch	hat gerochen	smell
ringen	ringt	rang	hat gerungen	wrestle
rufen	ruft	rief	hat gerufen	call
salzen	salzt	salzte	hat gesalzen	salt
saufen	säuft	soff	hat gesoffen	drink (animal)
schaffen	schafft	schuf	hat geschaffen	create, accomplish
scheiden	scheidet	schied	hat/ist geschieden	separate
scheinen	scheint	schien	hat geschienen	shine, seem
schieben	schieb	schob	hat geschoben	shove, push
schiessen	schiesst	schoss	hat geschossen	shoot
schlafen	schläft	schlief	hat geschlafen	sleep
schlagen	schlägt	schlug	hat geschlagen	hit, beat
schleichen	schleicht	schlich	ist geschlichen	creep
schliessen	schliesst	schloss	hat geschlossen	close, end
schmeissen	schmeisst	schmiss	hat geschmissen	throw out, chuck
schmelzen	schmilzt	schmolz	hat geschmolzen	melt
schneiden	schneidet	schnitt	hat geschnitten	cut
schreiben	schreibt	schrieb	hat geschrieben	write
schreien	schreit	schrie	hat geschrien	scream, shout
schreiten	schreitet	schritt	ist geschritten	stride
schweigen	schweigt	schwieg	hat geschwiegen	be silent
schwimmen	schwimmt	schwamm	hat/ist geschwommen	swim
schwingen	schwingt	schwang	ist geschwungen	swing
sehen	sieht	sah	hat gesehen	see
sein	ist	war	ist gewesen	be
senden	sendet	sandte	hat gesandt	send, deploy
singen	singt	sang	hat gesungen	sing
sinken	sinkt	sank	hat gesunken	sink
sitzen	sitzt	saß	hat gesessen	sit
sollen	soll	sollte	hat gesollt	should, supposed to
spinnen	spinnt	span	hat gesponnen	be silly, tell tall tales
sprechen	spricht	sprach	hat gesprochen	speak

INFINITIVE	PRESENT TENSE THIRD PERSON SINGULAR	PAST TENSE FIRST AND THIRD PERSONS SINGULAR	PAST PARTICIPLE WITH HELPING VERB	ENGLISH MEANING
springen	springt	sprang	ist gesprungen	jump, spring
stechen	sticht	stach	hat gestochen	stick, prick
stehen	steht	stand	hat gestanden	stand
stehlen	stiehlt	stahl	hat gestohlen	steal
steigen	steigt	stieg	ist gestiegen	climb
sterben	stirbt	starb	ist gestorben	die
stinken	stinkt	stank	hat gestunken	smell bad
stossen	stösst	stiess	hat/ist gestossen	bump, push
streichen	streicht	strich	hat gestrichen	stroke, pet, paint
streiten	streitet	stritt	hat gestritten	quarrel, argue
tragen	trägt	trug	hat getragen	carry, wear
treffen	trifft	traf	hat getroffen	meet
treiben	treibt	trieb	hat getrieben	drive
trinken	trinkt	trank	hat getrunken	drink
tun	tut	tat	hat getan	do
verbieten	verbietet	verbot	hat verboten	forbid
verderben	verdirbt	verdarb	hat/ist verdorben	spoil
vergessen	vergisst	vergass	hat vergessen	forget
verlieren	verliert	verlor	hat verloren	lose
verzeihen	verzeiht	verzieh	hat verzogen	forgive
wachsen	wächst	wuchs	ist gewachsen	grow
waschen	wäscht	wusch	hat gewaschen	wash
weichen	weicht	wich	ist gewichen	yield
weisen	weist	wies	hat gewiesen	point
werben	wirbt	warb	hat geworben	advertise
werden	wird	wurde	ist geworden	become, will
werfen	wirft	warf	hat geworfen	throw
wiegen	wiegt	wog	hat gewogen	weigh
wissen	weiss	wusste	hat gewusst	know (a fact)
wollen	will	wollte	hat gewollt	want, want to
ziehen	zieht	zog	hat gezogen	pull
zwingen	zwingt	zwang	hat gezwungen	force

5.   Definite and Indefinite Articles

DEFINITE ARTICLES

	SINGULAR			PLURAL
	MASCULINE	FEMININE	NEUTER	
NOMINATIVE	der	die	das	die
DATIVE	dem	der	dem	den
ACCUSATIVE	den	die	das	die

INDEFINITE ARTICLES

	SINGULAR			PLURAL
	MASCULINE	FEMININE	NEUTER	
NOMINATIVE	ein	eine	ein	keine
DATIVE	einem	einer	einem	keinen
ACCUSATIVE	einen	eine	ein	keine

6.   Adjective Endings

COMPARISON OF WEAK, STRONG, AND MIXED ADJECTIVE ENDINGS

	SINGULAR			PLURAL
	MASCULINE	FEMININE	NEUTER	
NOM. WEAK	der alt-e	die alt-e	das alt-e	die alt-en
MIXED	ein alt-er	eine alt-e	ein alt-es	keine alt-en
STRONG	alt-er	alt-e	alt-es	alt-e
DAT. WEAK	dem alt-en	der alt-en	dem alt-en	den alt-en
MIXED	einem alt-en	einer alt-en	einem alt-en	keinen alt-en
STRONG	alt-em	alt-er	alt-em	alt-en
ACC. WEAK	den alt-en	die alt-e	das alt-e	die alt-en
MIXED	einen alt-en	eine alt-e	ein alt-es	keine alt-en
STRONG	alt-en	alt-e	alt-es	alt-e
GEN. WEAK	des alt-en	der alt-en	des alt-en	der alt-en
MIXED	eines alt-en	einer alt-e	eines alt-en	keiner alt-en
STRONG	alt-en	alt-er	alt-en	alt-er

German-English Vocabulary

Abbreviations used in this glossary

acc. accusative

dat. inf.—informal

fam. familiar

fem. feminine

pl. plural

pol. polite

prep. dat./prep. acc. preposition which takes the dative/accusative case

sep. separable prefix

v.i. intransitive verb (verb that cannot take a direct object and usually uses sein to form the perfect tenses)

v.t. transitive verb (verb that can take a direct object and usually uses haben to form the perfect tenses)

A

ab from; up

der Abend, *pl.* **-e** evening

abends in the evening

aber but

abfahren, fährt ab, fuhr ab, ist abgefahren *sep.* to drive away

abholen *sep.* to pick up

acht eight

achtzehn eighteen

achtzig eighty

der Afrika Africa

aktiv active

alle all

allein alone

der Alligator, *pl.* **-en** alligator

alt old

altmodish old fashioned

am at; up; to *(dat.)*

der Amerikaner, *pl.* **-** American male

an at; up; up to; on

anfangen, fängt an, fing an, hat angefangen *sep.* to begin

die Angst, *pl.* **-e** worry; anxiety; fear

das Anorak, *pl.* **-s** anorak

anrufen, ruft an, rief an, hat angerufen *sep.* to call up

ansehen, sieht an, sah an, hat angesehen *sep.* to look at

die Antilope, *pl.* **-n** antilope

die Antwort, *pl.* **-en** answer

antworten to answer

der Anzug, *pl.* **-e** suit

der Apfel, *pl.* **-e** apple

der Apfelkuchen, *pl.* apple cake

die Apotheke, *pl.* **-en** drug store

der Apotheker, *pl.* **-** male pharmacist

die Apothekerin, *pl.* **-nen** female pharmacist

die Arbeit, *pl.* **-en** work

arbeiten to work

der Arm, *pl.* **-e** arm

die Armbanduhr, *pl.* **-en** wrist watch

der Arzt, *pl.* **-e** male doctor

die Ärztin, *pl.* **-nen** female doctor

das Asien Asia

auf up; on; onto

aufgeben *sep.* to give up

aufheben *sep.* to pick up

aufräumen *sep.* to clean up

aufstehen, steht auf, stand auf, ist aufgestanden *sep.* to stand up

das Auge, *pl.* **-n** eye

aus out; from; out of

ausgehen, geht aus, ging aus, ist ausgegangen *sep.* to go out

ausser, except for; with the exception of

aussprechen, spricht aus, sprach aus, hat ausgesprochen *sep.* to pronounce

das Auto, *pl.* **-s** car

automatisch automatic

B

das Baby, *pl.* **-s** baby

backen, bäckt, backte, hat gebacken *sep.* to bake

der Bäcker, *pl.* **-** baker

die Bäckerei, *pl.* **-en** bakery

der **Bahnhof**, *pl.* -e train station

der **Ball**, *pl.* ¨e ball

die **Banane**, *pl.* -n banana

die **Bank**, *pl.* -en/¨e bank; bench

der **Basketball**, *pl.* ¨e basketball

die **Batterie**, *pl.* -n battery

der **Baum**, *pl.* ¨e tree

beenden end

beginnen, beginnt, begann, hat begonnen to begin

bei at; near *(prep. dat.)*, at the home of

das **Bein**, *pl.* -e leg

bequem comfortable

der **Berater**, *pl.* - male advisor

die **Beraterin**, *pl.* -nen female advisor

der **Bericht**, *pl.* -e report

besonders especially

besorgen to get; to buy

besten to show up; to best

der **Besuch**, *pl.* -e visit

besuchen *v.t.* to visit

das **Bett**, *pl.* en bed

die **Bibliothek**, *pl.* -en library

der **Bibliothekar**, *pl.* - male librarian

die **Bibliothekarin**, *pl.* -nen female librarian

das **Bild**, *pl.* -er picture

bis *prep. acc.* until; up to

bitte please

blau blue

blauäugig blue-eyed

bleiben, bleibt, blieb, ist geblieben to stay

der **Bleistift**, *pl.* -e pencil

blonde blinde

die **Blume**, *pl.* -n flower

das **Blumengeschäft**, *pl.* -e florist; flower shop

die **Bluse**, *pl.* -n blouse

der **Bonbon**, *pl.* -s candy; sweet

braun brown

der **Braunbär**, *pl.* -en brown bear

die **Braut**, *pl.* ¨e bride

breit wide

die **Brille**, *pl.* -n eyeglasses

bringen, bringt, brachte, hat gebracht to bring

das **Brot**, *pl.* -e bread

der **Bruder**, *pl.* ¨ brother

brunette brunette

das **Buch**, *pl.* ¨er book

die **Buchhandlung**, *pl.* -en bookstore

der **Buchladen**, *pl.* ¨e book shop

bummeln to stroll

der **Bus**, *pl.* -se bus

die **Busfahrerin**, *pl.* -nen female bus driver

die **Busfahrt**, *pl.* -en bus trip

die **Butter** butter

C

die **CD**, *pl.* -s CD

CD-Laden, *pl.* ¨ CD shop

chinesisch Chinese

der **Chor**, *pl.* ¨e chorus

die **Cola**, *pl.* - cola

die **Couch**, *pl.* -es couch

der **Cousin**, *pl.* -s male cousin

die **Cousine**, *pl.* -n female cousin

D

der **Dank** thanks

danken to thank

dann then

das the *(ne)*

dass that

dazu for that; to it; to them

die **Decke**, *pl.* -n cover

decken to cover; to lay; to set

dein your *(fam.)*

dem the *(dat.)*

den the *(acc.)*

der the

das **Deutsch** German language

das **Deutschbuch**, *pl.* ¨er German book

der **Deutschklubfreund**, *pl.* -e German club member

das **Deutschland** Germany

der **Deutschlehrer**, *pl.* - male German teacher

dich you *(fam. acc.)*

dick thick; fat

die the *(fem; pl.)*

der **Dienstag**, *pl.* -e Tuesday

dir to you *(fam. dat.)*

der **Donnerstag**, *pl.* -e Thursday

dort there

dort drüben over there

drei three

dreissig thiry

dreizehn thirteen

dritt in threes

du you *(fam.)*

der **Duft**, *pl.* ¨e fragrance

dunkel dark; deep

durch *prep. acc.* through

dürfen, darf, durfte, hat gedurft to be allowed to; to be permitted; may

der **Durst** thirst

dynamisch dynamic

E

echt pure; genuine

die **Ecke**, *pl.* -n corner

ehrlich honest

das **Ei**, *pl.* -er egg

Eile haben to be in a hurry

ein a, an

einkaufen to go shopping

einladen, lädt ein, lud ein, hat eingeladen *sep.* to invite

eins one

der **Eisbär**, *pl.* -en polar bear

das **Eiscafé**, *pl.* -s ice cream parlor

der **Eistee**, *pl.* -s iced tea

der **Elefant**, *pl.* -en elephant

elf eleven

die Eltern parents
das Ende, *pl.* **n** end
endlich finally
energisch energetic
der Engel, *pl.* **-** angel
das Englisch English
  language
der Enkel, *pl.* **-** grandson
die Entschuldigung, *pl.* **-en**
  apology; excuse
er he
die Erdbeermarmelade,
  pl. **-n** strawberry jam
der Erdkundelehrer, *pl.* **-**
  male geography teacher
erklären to explain
erst first; only
erzählen to tell
es it
essen, isst, ass, hat
  gegessen to eat
das Etui, *pl.* **-s** pencil case
etwas something; anything
euch you
euer your *(fam. pl.)*

F
fahren, fährt, fuhr, ist/hat
  gefahren *v.i.* to drive
  away
Fahrplan, *pl.* **⁝e** timetable
Fahrrad, *pl.* **⁝er** bicycle
fallen, fällt, fiel, ist gefallen
  to fall
falsch wrong
die Familie, *pl.* **-n** family
fantastisch fantastic
die Farbe, *pl.* **-n** color
der Farbstift, *pl.* **-e** crayon
fehlen to be missing from
Feier, *pl.* **-n** celebration
der Fernfahrer, *pl.* **-** long
  distance driver
der Film, *pl.* **-e** film
finden, findet, fand, hat
  gefunden find
der Finger, *pl.* **-** finger
der Fisch, *pl.* **-e** fish

das Fleisch, *pl.* **-** meat
fliegen, fliegt, flog, ist
  geflogen to fly
die Flöte, *pl.* **-n** flute
folgen to follow
das Foto, *pl.* **-s** photograph
das Fragenspiel, *pl.* **-e** word
  game
die Französischlehrerin,
  pl. **-nen** female French
  teacher
die Frau, *pl.* **-en** woman
frei free
der Freitag, *pl.* **-e** Friday
fressen, frisst, frass, hat
  gefressen to eat
der Freund, *pl.* **-e** male friend
die Freundin, *pl.* **-nen**
  female friend
freundlich friendly
die Freundschaft, *pl.* **-en**
  friendship
froh happy
die Frucht, *pl.* **-e** fruit
das Frühstück, *pl.* **-e**
  breakfast
das Fundbüro, *pl.* **-s** lost
  and found
fünf five
fünfzehn fifteen
fünfzig fifty
für *prep. acc.* for
der Fussball, *pl.* **⁝e** soccer;
  soccer ball
der Fussballer, *pl.* **-** male
  soccer player
die Fussballerin, *pl.* **-nen**
  female soccer player
der Fussballtrainer, *pl.* **-**
  soccer coach

G
die Gabel, *pl.* **-n** fork
die Garage, *pl.* **-n** garage
der Garten, *pl.* **⁝** garden
die Gästeliste, *pl.* **-n** guest list
geben, gibt, gab, hat
  gegeben to give

die Geburtstagskarte, *pl.* **-n**
  birthday card
gefallen, gefällt, gefiel, hat
  gefallen to please; to be
  pleasing
der Gefangene, *pl.* **-n**
  prisoner
gegen against; around;
  about *(temporal)*
gehen, geht, ging, ist
  gegangen *v.i.* to go
gehorchen to obey
gehören to listen
gelb yellow
das Geld money
gemischt mixed
das Gemüse, *pl.* **-** vegetables
genau exactly; just
gepunktet polka dotted
gern gladly; with pleasure
das Geschäft, *pl.* **-e** store
geschehen to happen
die Geschichte, *pl.* **-n** story;
  history
die Geschichtslehrerin,
  pl. **-nen** female history
  teacher
das Geschirr china; crockery
gestern yesterday
gestreift striped
gesund healthy
das Getränk, *pl.* **-e** drink;
  beverage
gießen to pour
die Giraffe, *pl.* **-n** giraffe
das Glas, *pl.* **⁝er** glass
glauben to believe
gratulieren to congratulate
grau grey
gross large
die Grosseltern
  grandparents
die Großmutter, *pl.* **⁝**
  grandmother
der Großvater, *pl.* **⁝**
  grandfather
grün green
der Gruß, *pl.* **⁝e** greeting

grüßen to greet
der Gummistiefel, *pl.* -
rubber boot
der Gürtel, *pl.* - belt
gut good; well

H
das Haar, *pl.* -e hair
**haben, hat, hatte, hat
gehabt** to have
Hallo hello
die Halskette, *pl.* -n necklace
die Hand, *pl.* ¨e hand
der Handball, *pl.* ¨e handball
hart hard
hassen to hate
hast have
hat has
hatte had
die Hauptstraße, *pl.* -n main
street
das Haus, *pl.* ¨er house
die Hausaufgabe, *pl.* -n
homework
das Heft, *pl.* ¨e exercise book
der Heimweg, *pl.* ¨e the way
home
heiss hot
**heissen, heisst, hiess, hat
geheissen** to be called
**helfen, hilft, half, hat
geholfen** to help
hell bright
der Helm, *pl.* -e helmet
das Hemd, *pl.* -en shirt
**herkommen, kommt her,
kam her, ist
hergekommen** *sep.* to
come here
der Herr, *pl.* -en gentleman;
sir
heute today
hier here
hilfsbereit helpful
hinten at the back; back there
hinter behind
der Hirsch, *pl.* -e deer
das Hobby, *pl.* -s hobby

hoch high
hören to hear
die Hose, *pl.* -n pants
das Hotel, *pl.* -s hotel
hübsch pretty
der Hund, *pl.* -e dog
hundert hundred
der Hunger hunger
der Hut, *pl.* ¨e hat

I
ich I
ihm (to) him
ihn him
ihnen to you, them
Ihnen to you (*pol.*), to them
ihr her, you (*fam. pl.*), their
Ihr your (*pol. pl.*)
im in (*dat.*)
immer always
in in; into
das Indien India
die Ingenieuerin, *pl.* -nen
female engineer
das Instrument, *pl.* -e
instrument
intelligent intelligent
interessant interesting
ist is

J
die Jacke, *pl.* -n jacket
das Jahr, *pl.* -e year
das Jahrbuch, *pl.* ¨er
yearbook
jeder each
jemand someone;
somebody; anyone
jetzt now
joggen to jog
jung young
der Junge, *pl.* -n young man;
boy

K
der Kaffee, *pl.* -s coffee
der Kalender, *pl.* - calendar
kalt cold

das Kamel, *pl.* -e camel
die Kamera, *pl.* -s camera
kaputt broken
kariert checkered
die Karte, *pl.* -n card
der Käse cheese
das Käsebrot, *pl.* -e cheese
sandwich
der Käsekuchen, *pl.* -
cheesecake
die Katze, -n cat
kaufen to buy
das Kaufhaus, *pl.* -er
department store
kein none, not a(n), not any
der Keks, *pl.* -e cookie
der Keller, *pl.* - cellar
kennen to know
kennenlernen *sep.* to meet
das Kind child
der Kinderarzt, *pl.* ¨e
pediatrician
das Kino, *pl.* -s movie theater
die Kinogasse, *pl.* -n theater
alley
der Kiosk, *pl.* -e kiosk
die Kirche, *pl.* n church
die Klasse, *pl.* -n class
die Klassenarbeit, *pl.* -en
classwork
der Klassenlehrer, *pl.* -
teacher
der Klassensprecher, *pl.* -
male class president
die Klassensprecherin, *pl.* -
nen female class president
das Klassenzimmer, *pl.* -
classroom
das Klavier, *pl.* -e piano
der Klavierunterricht, *pl.* -
piano lesson
das Kleid, *pl.* -er dress
das Kleidergeschäft, *pl.* -e
dress shop
die Kleidung, collective
wardrobe
klein small
die Kleinstadt, *pl.* ¨e town

der **Klempner,** *pl.* - male plumber

die **Klempnerin,** *pl.* -nen female plumber

klug clever

kochen to cook

kommen, kommt, kam, ist gekommen to come

die **Konditorei,** *pl.* -en café

können, kann, konnte, hat gekonnt to be able to; can

das **Konzert** concert

die **Kopfschmerzen (plural)** headache

der **Kragen,** *pl.* - collar

krank sick

das **Krankenhaus,** *pl.* ¨er hospital

die **Krankheit,** *pl.* -en sickness

die **Krawatte,** *pl.* -n tie

die **Kreide** chalk

kriegen to get

das **Krokodil,** *pl.* -e crocodile

die **Küche,** *pl.* -n kitchen

der **Kuchen,** *pl.* - cake

das **Kuckucksnest,** *pl.* -er cuckoo's nest

die **Kuh,** *pl.* ¨e cow

kühl cool

der **Kuli,** *pl.* -e ballpoint pen

die **Kunsthochschule,** *pl.* -n art high school

der **Kunstlehrer,** *pl.* - male art teacher

die **Kunstlehrerin,** *pl.* -nen female art teacher

kurz short

L

der **Laden,** *pl.* ¨ shop

das **Land,** *pl.* ¨er country

lang long

die **Länge,** *pl.* -n length

langsam slow

langweilig boring

laufen, läuft, lief, ist gelaufen to run

laut loud

die **Lederjacke,** *pl.* -n leather jacket

der **Lehrer,** *pl.* - male teacher

die **Lehrerin,** *pl.* -nen female teacher

leid tun, tut leid, tat leid, hat leid getan to be sorry

leihen to borrow; to lend

lesen, liest, las, hat gelesen *v.t.* to read

letzt last

lieb love

das **Lied,** *pl.* -er song

lila mauve; lavender

die **Limonade,** *pl.* -n lemonade

das **Lineal,** *pl.* -e ruler

links left, to the left

die **Liste,** *pl.* -n list

der **Löffel,** *pl.* - spoon

der **Löwe,** *pl.* -n lion

der **Luftballon,** *pl.* -s balloon

die **Lüge,** *pl.* -n lie

die **Lust** pleasure; desire

Lust haben to like to do something

lustig cheerful

M

machen *v.t.* to make, to do

die **Macht** power

das **Mädchen,** *pl.* - girl

mähen to mow

manchmal sometimes

der **Mann,** *pl.* ¨er man

der **Mantel,** *pl.* ¨ coat

die **Mappe,** *pl.* -n portfolio, bag

der **Marktplatz,** *pl.* ¨e marketplace

die **Marmelade,** *pl.* -n jam

die **Mathe** math

die **Mathehausaufgabe,** *pl.* -n math homework

der **Mathelehrer,** *pl.* - male math teacher

die **Medizin,** *pl.* -en medicine

mein my

das **Messer,** *pl.* - knife

der **Meter,** *pl.* - meter

die **Metzgerei,** *pl.* -en butcher shop

mich me

die **Milch** milk

mir to me, from me

mit with; along

der **Mitarbeiter,** *pl.* - partner

mitbringen, bringt mit, brachte mit, hat mitgebracht *sep.* to bring with

der **Mitschüler,** *pl.* - male classmate

der **Mittag,** *pl.* -e noon

die **Mittagspause,** *pl.* -n lunch break

die **Mitte,** *pl.* - middle

der **Mittwoch,** *pl.* -e Wednesday

möchten to like; to like to

mögen, mag, mochte, hat gemocht to be allowed to; may

der **Moment,** *pl.* -e moment

der **Montag,** *pl.* -e Monday

morgen tomorrow

der **Morgen,** *pl.* - morning

müde tired

das **Museum,** *pl.* die **Museen** museum

die **Musik** music

der **Musiklehrer,** *pl.* - male music teacher

müssen, muss, musste, hat gemusst to have to, must

das **Muster,** *pl.* - sample; model

die **Mutter,** *pl.* ¨ mother

die **Mütze,** *pl.* -n cap

N

nach after; to (with geographic location)

nachkommen, kommt nach, kam nach, ist nachgekommen *sep.* to come after

nass wet
neben beside; next to; near
nett nice
neu new; young
neugierig curious
neun nine
neunzehn nineteen
neunzig ninety
nicht not
die Nichte, *pl.* **-n** niece
das Nilpferd, *pl.* **-e**
  hippopotamus
noch still, yet
die Note, *pl.* **-n** mark; grade
die Nudel, *pl.* **-n** noodle
der Nudelsalat, *pl.* **-e** noodle
  salad
nur only

O
das Obst fruit
oder or
öffnen, *v.t.* to open
oft often
ohne without
die Omas Grandma
der Onkel, *pl.* **-** uncle
der Opas grandpa
die Oper, *pl.* **-n** opera
orange orange
der Orangensaft, *pl.* **¨e**
  orange juice
das Orchester, *pl.* **-**
  orchestra
das Österreich Austria

P
das Paket, *pl.* **-e** packet
das Papier, *pl.* **-e** paper
der Park, *pl.* **-s** park
parken to park
die Party, *pl.* **-s** party
das Partyzimmer, *pl.* **-** party
  room
passieren to happen
das Pausebrot, *pl.* **-e** snack
perfekt perfect
das Pferd, *pl.* **-e** horse
die Pflanze plant

der Pilot, *pl.* **-** male pilot
die Pilotin *pl.* **-nen** female
  pilot
die Pizza, *pl.* **-s, Pizzen**
  pizza
das Polen Poland
der Polizist, *pl.* **-en**
  policeman
die Polizistin, *pl.* **-nen**
  female police officer
die Post collective mail;
  post office
die Postkarte, *pl.* **-n**
  postcard
prima great
das Problem, *pl.* **-e** problem
der Professor, *pl.* **-en** male
  professor
die Professorin, *pl.* **-nen**
  female professor
der Pulli, *pl.* **-s** sweater
die Puppe, *pl.* **-n** doll

R
das Rad, *pl.* **¨er** bike
der Rasen, *pl.* **-** lawn
das Rathaus, *pl.* **¨er** town
  hall
rauchen to smoke
rechts right
der Regenmantel, *pl.* **¨**
  raincoat
der Regenschirm, *pl.* **-e**
  umbrella
regnen to rain
der Rektor, *pl.* **-en**
  headmaster; principal
rennen, rennt, rannte, ist
  gerannt to run
das Restaurant, *pl.* **-s**
  restaurant
richtig correct
der Ring, *pl.* **-e** ring
der Rock, *pl.* **¨** skirt
die Rockmusik rock
  music
rosa pink
rot red
ruhig quiet

S
die Sache, *pl.* **-n** thing
der Saft, *pl.* **¨e** juice
sagen to say
der Salat, *pl.* **-e** salad
der Samstag, *pl.* **-e** Saturday
der Samstagsmarkt, *pl.* **¨e**
  Saturday market
das Schach chess
die Schachmeisterin,
  pl. **-nen** female chess pro
schaden to harm
der Schal, *pl.* **die Schals**
  scarf
das Schaufenster, *pl.* **-**
  display window
der Schauspieler, *pl.* **-** actor
die Schauspielerin, *pl.* **-nen**
  actress
schenken to give a gift
schick chic; stylish
das Schild, *pl.* **-er** sign
schlafen, schläft, schlief,
  hat geschlafen to sleep
der Schlafsack, *pl.* **¨e**
  sleeping bag
schlampig sloppy
die Schlange, *pl.* **-n** snake
schlank thin
schlecht bad
schnell fast
der Schnellimbiss, *pl.* **-e** fast
  food stand
der Schokoladenkuchen,
  pl. **-** chocolate cake
die Schokoladentorte, *pl.* **-n**
  chocolate cake with icing
schon already
schön beautiful
schreiben, schreibt, schrieb,
  hat geschrieben, *v.t.* to
  write
schreien, schreit, schrie, hat
  geschrien to scream
der Schreibtisch, *pl.* **-e** desk
der Schuh, *pl.* **-e** shoe
der Schulbus, *pl.* **-se**
  schoolbus
die Schule, *pl.* **-n** school

der **Schüler**, *pl.* - male student

die **Schülerin**, *pl.* -nen female student

das **Schulfest**, *pl.* die **Schulfeste** school festival

die **Schulsachen**, *pl.* - school supplies

der **Schultag**, *pl.* -e school day

die **Schultasche**, *pl.* -n bookbag

das **Schulzeugnis**, *pl.* -se report card

schwarz black

das **Schwein**, *pl.* -e pig

die **Schweiz** Switzerland

die **Schwester**, *pl.* -n sister

das **Schwimmbad**, *pl.* -er swimming pool

schwimmen, schwimmt, schwamm, ist geschwommen, *v.i.* to swim

sechs six

sechzehn sixteen

sechzig sixty

sehen, sieht, sah, hat gesehen to see

sehr very

seid (you) are *pol. and inf.* (you) are

sein, ist, war, ist gewesen to be

seit since *(temporal)*

setzen to set, put

die **Shorts** shorts

sie she, they

Sie you *(pol.)*

sieben seven

siebzehn seventeen

siebzig seventy

sind are

singen, singt, sang, hat gesungen to sing

sitzen, sitzt, sass, hat gesessen to sit

die **Socke**, *pl.* -n sock

das **Sofa**, *pl.* -s sofa

der **Sohn**, *pl.* -e son

der **Soldat**, *pl.* -en male soldier

die **Soldatin**, *pl.* -nen female soldier

sollen, soll, sollte, hat gesollt should; to be supposed to

die **Sommerjacke**, *pl.* -n summer jacket

der **Sonntag**, *pl.* -e Sunday

der **Sonntagnachmittag,** *pl.* -e Sunday afternoon

die **Spaghetti** spaghetti

das **Spanisch** Spanish

der **Spanischlehrer**, *pl.* - male Spanish teacher

der **Spaß**, *pl.* -e fun; joke

spät late

spazieren to walk

das **Spiel**, *pl.* -e game

das **Spielauto**, *pl.* -s toy car

spielen to play

die **Spielkarten** playing cards

der **Spielplatz**, *pl.* -e playground

der **Spielraum**, *pl.* -e playroom

die **Spitze**, *pl.* -n point; top

der **Sport** sport

das **Sportgeschäft**, *pl.* -e sporting goods store

die **Sporthalle**, *pl.* -n sports arena

Sportlehrerin, *pl.* -nen female phys. ed. teacher

die **Sportlerin**, *pl.* -nen female sports figure

sportlich sporty

der **Sportplatz**, *pl.* -e stadium

sprechen, spricht, sprach, hat gesprochen to speak

springen, springt, sprang to jump

spülen to rinse; to water

die **Stadt**, *pl.* -e city

der **Stadtpark**, *pl.* -s city park

das **Stadttheater**, *pl.* - city theater

der **Stammbaum**, *pl.* -e family tree

der **Stoff**, *pl.* -e fabric

die **Straße**, *pl.* -n street

der **Student**, *pl.* - male university student

die **Studentin**, *pl.* -nen female university student

der **Stuhl**, *pl.* -e chair

der **Stundenanfang**, *pl.* -e beginning of class

super super

der **Supermarkt**, *pl.* -e supermarket

die **Suppe**, *pl.* -n soup

süss sweet

das **Symbol**, *pl.* -e symbol

T

die **Tafel**, *pl.* -n blackboard

der **Tag**, *pl.* -e day

das **Talent**, *pl.* -e talent

die **Tankstelle**, *pl.* -n gas station

die **Tante**, *pl.* -n aunt

tanzen to dance

die **Tasche**, *pl.* -n pocket; bag

die **Taxifahrerin**, *pl.* -nen female taxi driver

die **Teamliste**, *pl.* -n team list

der **Teddybär**, *pl.* -en Teddy bear

teilen to share; to divide

der **Tennisball**, *pl.* -e tennis ball

die **Tennisklasse**, *pl.* -n tennis class

das **Tennistraining**, *pl.* - tennis training

der **Termin**, *pl.* -e date; appointment

der **Tiger**, *pl.* - tiger

der **Tisch**, *pl.* -e table

die **Tochter**, *pl.* -e daughter
toll great
die **Tomatensoße**, *pl.* -n
   tomato sauce
die **Torte**, *pl.* -n cake
die **Tour**, *pl.* -en tour
tragen, trägt, trug, hat
   getragen to wear; to carry
der **Trainer**, *pl.* - trainer
die **Trompete**, *pl.* -n trumpet
Tschüs bye-bye
das **T-Shirt**, *pl.* -s T-shirt
tun to do
die **Tür**, *pl.* -en door

U
üben to practice; to exercise
über over; about; above;
   across
die **Übung**, *pl.* -en lesson
die **Uhr**, *pl.* -en clock
um at; up to
und and
die **Uni**, *pl.* -s university
uns us, to us
unser our
unter under
unvollendet unfinished

V
der **Vater**, *pl.* ⁀e father
verantwortungsvoll
   responsible
die **Vergangenheit** past
vergessen, vergisst, vergass,
   hat vergessen to forget
verzeihen to forgive
das **Videospiel**, *pl.* -e video
   game
viel much
viele many
vier four
vierzehn fourteen
vierzig forty

der **Volleyball**, *pl.* ⁀e
   volleyball
das **Vollkornbrot**, *pl.* -e
   whole grain bread
von from, of
vor before; in front of
vorlesen, liest vor, las vor, hat
   vorgelesen to read aloud
vorn, vorne at the front

W
der **Wald**, *pl.* ⁀er forest
der **Waldweg**, *pl.* -e forest
   path
wann when
war was
warm warm
warten to wait
warum why
was what
die **Wäsche**, *pl.* -n wash;
   laundry
weg away; off; gone
wehtun, tut weh, tat weh,
   hat wehgetan *sep.* to do
   harm; to hurt
weil because
weiss white
weit far
weiter farther; further
die **Welt**, *pl.* -en world
wer who
werden, wird, wurde, ist
   geworden (become) to
   become
wessen whose
das **Wettrennen**, *pl.* -
   contest, race
wie how
wiederholen to repeat
der **Wintermantel**, *pl.* ⁀
   winter coat
wir we
das **Wissen** knowledge

wissen, weiß, wusste, hat
   gewusst to know
die **Woche**, *pl.* -n week
das **Wochenende**, *pl.* -n
   weekend
woher from where
wohin where to
wohnen to live
die **Wohnung**, *pl.* -en
   apartment
der **Wolf**, *pl.* die **Wölfe** wolf
wollen, will, wollte, hat
   gewollt to want; to want
   to
das **Wort**, *pl.* ⁀er word
das **Worträtsel**, *pl.* - word
   puzzle
der **Wortschatz** vocabulary
wunderbar wonderful
wünschen to wish
die **Wurst**, *pl.* ⁀e sausage
das **Wurstbrot**, *pl.* -e
   sausage sandwich

Z
das **Zebra**, *pl.* -s zebra
zehn ten
zeigen to show
das **Zelt**, *pl.* -e tent
das **Zimmer**, *pl.* - bedroom
die **Zitronenbutter** lemon
   butter
der **Zoo**, *pl.* - zoo
zu to; toward
zuerst first of all
zuhören, *v.t.* to listen to
zuletzt in the end, finally
zurück back
zwanzig twenty
zwei two
der **Zwilling**, *pl.* -e twin
zwischen between
zwölf twelve